FRONT ROW ON DEATH ROW

Conversations with Convicted Killers

Steve Schonveld

Our Accent is Southern!

© 2021 Steve Schonveld

All rights reserved. No part of this book may be reproduced or transmitted in any form or by any means, electronic or mechanical, including photocopying, recording, or by any information storage and retrieval system, without permission in writing from the copyright owner.

Schonveld, Steve. Front Row on Death Row: Conversations with Convicted Killers
Published by Evening Post Books, Charleston, South Carolina.

ISBN-13: 978-1-929647-53-8

Cover and interior design by Michael J. Nolan

Cover photo by Grace Beahm Alford, *Charleston Post and Courier*

Acknowledgments

Writing a book is hard work and by no means did I do this by myself. It takes a full team and I had a great squad. None of this would have been possible without Ron Burris. Thank you, Ron, for trusting me to tell your story and our journey. You have changed the way I think about prisons, prisoners, and people in general. Your story is remarkable, uplifting, powerful, and inspiring. I'm proud to call you a friend.

Thank you to the team at Evening Post Books, especially Michael Nolan and John Burbage. You took a chance on a first-time author and I appreciate you believing in me and the power of my story. You allowed me to carry out the vision I had for this book and guided me gracefully in the right direction.

Thank you to my family. Most family members will always tell you that your writings and stories are good, and my family is no exception, but you all were not afraid to tell me when something didn't make sense or didn't quite fit. I needed that and I truly appreciated your honest feedback. When I mentioned that I come from a long line of people who give a damn about other people, you four are the people I was referring to. I love you all.

To Mark Peper, thank you for having my back when I needed it. I often needed advice on how to move forward and you always took my call.

Thank you to everyone who encouraged me to write a book. It never crossed my mind until several of you told me that I should. That's a saying you hear a lot when you have a good story to tell… "You should write a book!" I didn't take it seriously until many of you persistently said, "No, seriously, you need to write a book." Thank you for the encouragement and support.

Dedication

To Mom and Dad,

Turns out you were right;

Reading is cool.

Prologue

We want the facts to fit the preconceptions. When they don't it is easier to ignore the facts than to change the preconceptions.

Jessamyn West

It's true that dead men tell no tales, but dead men walking do. I hope you appreciate these stories about the men I got to know who live on South Carolina's death row. I also hope that, free of preconceived notions, you gain a better understanding of the dark world of doomed men who do little more than exist day after day behind bars awaiting their fates.

As you read what I have to say you might find yourself relating to them as people instead of monsters, but you don't have to admit it to anyone. If asked, you could say you have empathy, not sympathy, for them. But I think it best to understand the difference between these two words, which are often misused interchangeably. "Sympathy" is a feeling of compassion, sorrow and/or pity for someone. "Empathy" is the ability to put oneself in the place of the troubled other and understand to some degree what he or she is going through.

Throughout this book, there will be times when you'll think, "That killer is on death row for a reason and deserves what he's going through." I often had that thought while talking to them, and wrestled with myself before, during, and after the encounters. But I realized that for me it was not about sympathy. So, to understand what I'm offering here, try to focus on empathy — what it's like to live without any real degree of freedom in a one-man prison cell for days, weeks, and years until you die.

If you don't feel sorry for them, that's understandable, and you are not alone. Most people have no sympathy for murderers awaiting their fates on death row. Most people have never been there and never will. However, it's important as well as healthy to allow yourself to feel something. I'm convinced that if you read this book objectively, you will be moved in some way. Also, for the record, I feel no sympathy for any of the men I met on numerous visits to South Carolina's death row. They made their prison beds, and they deserve to lie in them.

I did not write this book with the intention of persuading anyone to either support or oppose the death penalty. I consider it a private, very personal decision. I spoke with 34 of the 37 criminals condemned to die by the state of South Carolina. I did not talk to any death penalty experts — pro, con, or neutral on the subject. I have not collaborated with anyone who has visited death row except for my friend Ron, who I will soon introduce to you. That was intentional. I'm telling you my story the way I see it, and my thoughts and reflections are authentic and honest.

Most of us tend to write off others with points of view different than our own, especially if we have little or nothing in common. That's because humans are generally shortsighted and divided on many matters. We too often argue while standing tall for what we believe and fail to listen carefully, if at all, to other points of view. When people do this, conversation typically becomes a competition to determine who can talk loudest and longest. And while winning a yelling match can be invigorating, it is seldom productive. I'd rather try to appeal thoughtfully to hearts, not heads, when discussing such controversial matters. I've learned that when you reach the heart, the head reacts responsibly.

I also think that people from different backgrounds, and with few if any life experiences in common, can get along. Indeed, the death row inmates with whom I disagreed on some things and agreed on others understand this. They were respectful to me, as was I to them.

I had never been inside a prison before I set foot in Lieber Correctional Institute, which is located in Dorchester County not far from Summerville. I've never been arrested or detained by the police. I once got caught drinking in high school, and the consequences of that were five days of suspension and 10 hours of community service at a local outreach center where I helped the oldest woman on Earth collate papers. My only source of information about prison behavior and inmate conduct had been cable television.

I watched the documentary film *Scared Straight*, and admit that, while inside the prison, I worried that Brutus might corner me one day and give me an earful about what my life could be like if I didn't listen to my parents and teachers and got into trouble with the law. Watching television's *Lockup* series convinced me that I never wanted to spend time in jail — especially as some burly guy's wife. That's about all I knew about prison life before I first set foot in death row. When I did, I entered what immediately became obvious — extremely foreign territory.

Upon arrival at the prison, I walked through an airport-like security line, received two pat-downs, handed over my driver's license, watch, and car keys, and proceeded through a succession of steel doors through an area housing the general prison population to the maximum security section and then to death row. No guards walked behind me, no corrections officers were strategically placed on the tiers and standing watch. What if something awful happened?

As I approached each corner inside death row I had no idea who or what was waiting for me. All I was told is not to get too close to the cells, which wasn't easy. Almost all the inmates stuck out their hands to shake mine as I passed. Leaving someone hanging, no matter who it is, goes against the unwritten rules of engagement.

Each man was in a separate cell — caged like a dangerous animal. I noticed a few of them standing at their doors, their faces pressed against steel bars. Looking down the halls, I saw mostly elbows to fingertips protruding through the food slots — a very strange scene. I snapped mental pictures of everything: the peeling floor; the buckets that caught water dripping from the ceiling; the two tiny TV sets mounted high in corners of the common area, a room that no inmates have been allowed to enter for years; the loud industrial fans blowing hot and humid air; the showers surrounded by bars; the cell that serves as a library lined wall to wall, floor to ceiling with books; the two guards sitting inside the control room, between the two sections of death row; the microwave on a rolling cart for inmates to share; the pay phone on another rolling cart.

I moved cautiously and looked around each corner before making a turn. And, as I said, I did shake their hands:

— The hand of Mr. Aleksey. The same hand that killed a police officer during a traffic stop on Interstate 95. On death row since 1998.

— The hand of Mr. Allen. The same hand that pulled the trigger of a gun that killed four people, one of them sitting quietly on a bench — just for target practice. On death row since 2005.

— The hand of Mr. Bennett. The same hand that stabbed a man at least 70 times with a screwdriver until he was dead. On death row since 1995.

— The hand of Mr. Bell. The same hand that killed an elementary school principal who was walking to his car at night. (Bell was on the row for 28 years before his death sentence was overturned in 2017, three months after our last conversation. As of this writing, he is serving a life sentence at a different detention center in South Carolina.)

— The hand of Mr. Binney. The same hand that shot and killed a woman he'd never met before. He was also convicted of sexually assaulting his own infant daughter. On death row since 2001.

— The hand of Mr. Bixby. The same hand that killed two police officers. On death row since 2007.

— The hand of Mr. Blackwell. The same hand that shot and killed an eight-year-old girl. On death row since 2014.

— The hand of Mr. Bowman. The same hand that killed a woman and set her body on fire. On death row since 2001.

— The hand of Mr. S. Bryant. The same hand that shot four people and used their blood to write messages on the walls. On death row since 2004.

— The hand of Mr. J. Bryant. The same hand that killed a policeman during a traffic stop by overpowering the officer and using his own pistol against him. On death row since 2004.

— The hand of Mr. Cottrell. The same hand that shot a police officer in the face after being stopped on a sidewalk for questioning. On death row since 2005.

— The hand of Mr. Council. The same hand that tied up and tortured an elderly woman, forced her to drink household cleaners, and murdered her. On death row since 1996.

— The hand of Mr. Dickerson. The same hand that kidnapped, sexually assaulted, and killed the man he suspected of having sex with his girlfriend. Turns out the victim was the wrong man. On death row since 2009.

— The hand of Mr. Finklea. The same hand that set a security officer on fire while still alive, eventually killing him. Finklea was robbing an ATM at the time. On death row since 2007.

— The hand of Mr. Inman. The same hand that raped and murdered a Clemson engineering student. On death row since 2006.

— The hand of Mr. Jones. The same hand that raped and murdered both his ex-employer and wife. On death row since 1984.

— The hand of Mr. Lindsey. The same hand that killed his own wife while two young children watched. On death row since 2004.

— Mr. Mahdi was also in there. He shot a police officer nine times before setting him ablaze. He had been on the run for killing a gas station attendant. I never spoke to him because his cell was fenced off. No one like me could get within five feet of him. He had attempted to escape multiple times, tried to kill a prison employee, and somehow got possession of weapons. I made eye contact with

Mr. Mahdi but was warned not to engage in conversation with him — ever. On death row since 2004.

— The hand of Mr. Moore. The same hand that shot and killed a convenience store clerk. On death row since 2001.

— The hand of Mr. Northcutt. The same hand that beat his four-month-old daughter to death. On death row since 2003.

— Mr. Owens was also there. He killed a store clerk and later, while in prison, strangled a man to death. I didn't speak to Mr. Owens because he too was fenced off. He also assaulted prison employees with intent to kill, possessed weapons, damaged and destroyed property, threw bodily substances on others, and was an exhibitionist who masturbated in public. On death row since 2003.

— The hand of Mr. Roberts. The same hand that shot and killed two police officers while they searched his home. On death row since 2002.

— The hand of Mr. Robertson. The same hand that killed two people with a hammer and a baseball bat. On death row since 1999.

— The hand of Mr. Sigmon. The same hand that killed a man and woman by beating them with a baseball bat. On death row since 2002.

— The hand of Mr. Singleton. The same hand that killed an elderly woman. On death row since 1983.

— The hand of Mr. Stanko. The same hand that killed his live-in girlfriend, slit her 15-year-old daughter's throat, and killed a 74-year-old man, all in the span of two days. On death row since 2006.

— The hand of Mr. Starnes. The same hand that shot two men, and left their bodies in some woods. On death row since 1997.

— The hand of Mr. Stokes. The same hand that sexually assaulted then shot and killed a woman. On death row since 1999.

— The hand of Mr. Stone. The same hand that killed a police officer while he was breaking into a woman's home. On death row since 1996.

— The hand of Mr. Terry. The same hand that raped and beat a 47-year-old woman to death inside her home. On death row since 1997.

— The hand of Mr. Torres. The same hand that killed a man, and sexually assaulted and killed a woman. On death row since 2007.

— The hand of Mr. Weik. The same hand that murdered his ex-girlfriend in her home. On death row since 1999.

— The hand of Mr. Williams. The same hand that shot his ex-girlfriend inside a grocery store deli after holding her hostage for two hours. On death row since 2005.

— The hand of Mr. Winkler. The same hand that shot his estranged wife in the face in front of her 14-year-old son. On death row since 2008.

— The hand of Mr. Wood. The same hand that killed a police officer during a traffic stop after being pulled over while riding a moped. On death row since 2002.

— The hand of Mr. Woods. The same hand that raped and murdered a schoolteacher. On death row since 2006.

— I also saw Mr. Wilson, who shot and killed two eight-year-old girls inside an elementary school. I didn't shake his hand because his cell access window was always locked. I could see him, though, and he appeared to be mentally ill. He wore no clothes, his toilet was filled with feces and urine, and the stench was unbearable. He was like a snake, lying motionless most of the time. When he moved, I watched. On death row since 1989.

It's impossible for me to confirm that everything I was told is 100 percent accurate, but everything you read in this book is what I saw and heard in Lieber and on South Carolina's death row. Below is an aerial photo of the prison with labels showing where everything is located.

Chapter 1

Talking *about* killers and talking *to* killers is not the same. Interacting face to face, separated only by steel bars, is not easy either. Thirty-seven cold-blooded murderers and me — in their den, their comfort zone. I didn't belong there. The moment I first walked into death row, I stopped and simply observed for a minute. From my vantage point, I could see the entire left side of death row. It's about the size of five racquetball courts, with two tiers of single cells. The volume was surprisingly low…almost seemed too quiet. I didn't know at that moment just how much I would learn over the next six months.

I was nervous and intimidated, yet curious. What should I say? Would they initiate conversation? Would they even speak to me? They are caged, but they are not animals, I reminded myself. Most had been there for a very long time. Surely they'd like to have someone new to talk to.

I wondered what I would learn about those people. I had no idea then that I'd be back again and again for almost six months. I had no idea then what I'd learn about myself.

Getting inside death row was surprisingly simple. I'm an assistant principal of a kindergarten-through-eighth-grade school in Charleston. During the opening days of the school year, parent Ron Burris approached me as I stood in the main lobby greeting everyone before the morning bell. Parents were there to meet me, and the children were smiling, happy, and excited.

I was in a groove that morning, fist-bumping first-graders when Ron and his wife, Kim, introduced themselves. Ron is a happy, energetic man. He and Kim had two children enrolled at my school. He asked if I was interested in having an ex-convict talk to the students about drugs, violence, prison, and the like.

"Uh, I'm not sure about that," I said. "Do you know someone?"

"Yeah, me," he said. "I'm a felon. I've been on both sides of a gun, and I'd love to help out."

Ron had my attention. He started telling me about the police who had shot him multiple times, and he rolled up his sleeves to show the bullet wounds as we stood in the main lobby of my elementary school. Seven-year-olds were walking by and seeing us. I told Ron that I'd love to hear his story, but later, in the privacy of my office. He thanked me politely and moved on.

"How did he get past the security scanner in the front office?" I asked myself. "Should I have it replaced? Should I unplug it, and blow on it like it's 1991 and I'm trying to get my Nintendo game to work?"

Every school-day morning thereafter, Ron escorted his daughters through the front doors. Every morning, we'd say hello. One day he suggested that I Google his name and read the details, which I did. He had stolen a car on US Highway 17 and led the cops on a several-hour car chase spanning more than 200 miles. They shot at him 48 times and hit him 12.

The next time I saw him in the hallway, I asked him to join me in my office, where he told me what had happened: He was an ex-con. He stole a car. He didn't stop for the blue lights. He was shot multiple times and arrested not far from the school. After a lengthy recovery from his wounds and a trial, he served four and a half years behind bars, and subsequently volunteered with a prison ministries organization, mostly at Lieber, which is not far up the road from my school. He had served some of his sentence at Lieber, and was currently counseling inmates about forgiveness, responsibility, and such.

"I sometimes stop in on death row and talk to them quite a bit," he said.

I didn't know Lieber had a death row. Oddly enough, I've long been fascinated by prisons and how they work. I had watched a lot of prison shows on television. So I asked to join him. He was optimistic, saying all he had to do was get the prison chaplain to agree. He told me to email a copy of my driver's license to prison authorities, which I did, and soon afterward I was cleared to accompany the ministry team on an upcoming Friday. No training, no questionnaire, no signing off — nothing.

On September 23, 2016, I spent nearly 12 hours inside the thick walls of Lieber, a level 3 maximum-security prison that houses all of South Carolina's death row inmates (37 at that time), along with 1,200 other convicted criminals. Ron and I arrived at Lieber at 6 a.m., but were told to wait until after breakfast to enter the front gate. We sat outside on a bench. Sunrises aren't as enjoyable when the foreground is a maximum-security prison. At 7 a.m., the intake process began and I soon learned that my name was not on the list. So I explained that I was invited by the prison chaplain.

"Ok, just write him in," the guard told a lady sitting at a nearby desk. I was given a nametag and escorted through the first gate and walked about 50 yards to the next one. It was easier to get clearance there. Through that gate is the lobby — only five people allowed in there at a time. I checked in again at a third gate. Sitting behind a desk with plexiglass for protection was a woman who, I assume, was in charge of keeping the lobby under control. To the right of her was a hallway. Along the right side of it were a few occupied holding cells. I have no clue why the men in those cells were there. They were awake, so I'm guessing they hadn't been there long and weren't planning on staying. As I walked down the short hallway toward the exit gate, the inmates in those cells didn't smile or acknowledge me, but we did make eye contact. If it were a staring contest, I would have lost.

The chapel would be the next stop, I was told, but I had to cross a prison yard to get there. I was soon among lots of inmates wearing baggy, tan ensembles with SCDC (South Carolina Department of Corrections) inscribed across the back of each shirt and down the side of each pant leg. Inmates are not allowed to cross a yellow line painted down the middle of the walkway. I was careful to stay on the inmates' side of the line until Ron reminded me that I did not live there and the rule didn't apply to me.

We entered the chapel and were asked if we wanted coffee. I said yes and sat down at a table with another "layperson," as they call visitors, along with eight inmates. I was told earlier not to ask prisoners what they did to get there. I introduced myself and everyone at the table did the same. Most inmates gave only their last names. I could not help but wonder about their crimes but wasn't about to ask.

For the next two hours I attended various classroom-like sessions and listened to inmates and laypeople talk about forgiveness, love, friendship, and God. Between these sessions, we — visitors and inmates — were asked to discuss among ourselves the speakers' points of view. This was when the inmates were supposed to open up, but few of them did. The "pod leaders" did, though, and they were alarmingly honest. I was someone they had just met. They didn't know who I was or why I was there, but I sensed they appreciated my presence. I expected a lot of "just going through the motions" types of attitudes, but that's not at all what I experienced. They were sincere, genuine, and authentic.

I noticed that a few of the inmates had teardrops tattooed below their eyes. I later learned that it is a mark that has various meanings. In some prisons, a teardrop signifies that the wearer is a murderer. In others, it means he or she is serving a lengthy prison sentence. Teardrops sometimes mean that a friend was murdered and the wearer seeks revenge. Some teardrops were empty and others filled with ink. Regardless of the meaning, I knew it did not signify that the recipient of the teardrop tattoo below his eyeball was a model citizen who had been a high school valedictorian and altar boy prior to that.

The chaplain said inmates volunteer to join these sessions because, among other things, participation breaks the monotony. Authorities encourage leaders of various prison pods to join in because they have earned a degree of respect from other inmates and have influence on their neighbors. "Many have life sentences and will likely never get out. If they do, they'll be old men," the chaplain said.

I felt a little more comfortable as my first day behind bars progressed. I asked each inmate at my table what was the most shocking thing about prison he experienced after arriving at Lieber. One response was especially noteworthy: "I felt like I had helped so many people in my life. I was a football coach, a dad, a husband. I always put my family first. When I came here, they all shut me out. I couldn't wrap my head around the fact that after all I did for those people, they shut the door on me so quickly."

Multiple times throughout the day, extra guards arrived and announced: "Count time!" All the inmates at the table stood up, formed a straight line and counted out by name. The pods — or living units — at Lieber are named after the rivers in and around Charleston: Edisto, Cooper, Stono, Ashley, Wando. The guard called out the name of the pod followed by the inmate's last name — as in, "Edisto, Hamilton," then Hamilton would say, "Here." The process took about five minutes.

As I sat at the table, I made it a point to check out the windows — each only about five inches wide and somewhat longer. All I saw on the outside were brick walls and razor wire. Charleston is blessed with breathtaking views, and is regularly ranked as a top tourist destination in America by various travel magazines. I saw no evidence of that from my seat in the chapel — or anywhere else in the prison complex for that matter.

I asked about the prison canteen. The men at my table said they had seldom been to the canteen because they had no money, and that those who do have cash can get what they need from others out in the yard. A pound of tobacco sells for $2,000 and a cell phone is $750, although buying one is risky. It's likely the person who sold it will show up later with a few of his buddies and demand that you give it back. If you decline or put up a fight, "You'll take a trip."

"A trip? What does that mean?" I asked.

"It's a free ride in an ambulance to the hospital or the cemetery," I was told. "Mo' money; mo' problems."

Lunch was served at 11:30 a.m., and a rather large fellow sitting next to me ate a two-foot-long cold-cut sandwich. Afterward, a layperson named Tony tapped me on the shoulder: "You want to give the death row inmates some cookies?"

"Do they like it when you give them cookies?" I asked. "I don't want to do anything they won't like."

Tony chuckled: "They love cookies."

Soon, Tony, Chris (another layperson), and I exited the chapel with three plastic garbage bags full of cookies. Two bags were labeled "Max" and one was tagged "death row." We crossed the yard among the regular inmates, went through several gates, entered a building with a "Maximum Security" sign above the door, and walked down a long hallway painted stark white with skinny windows floor to ceiling.

I've jumped out of an airplane at 15,000 feet. I've snorkeled in shark-infested waters. I've never been as frightened as I was that day walking down that hallway. We passed a guard wearing a bulletproof vest and a firearm or a stun gun — I couldn't tell. We stopped at another gate, which had a red sign saying "Death Row." Tony looked at me and I looked at him.

"You're going to find that this a surprisingly relaxed place, Steve," he said.

Really? I thought. Then why do I feel the exact opposite of relaxed?

The heavy doors swung open as we approached as if someone was expecting us. On the other side stood two guards who greeted us and two more behind a control booth encased in what appeared to be a very thick glass.

"Empty your pockets, face the wall, and put your hands up," one guard said.

After patting us down they asked if we were ready. Tony must have said yes. I certainly did not.

There are two sections of death row: one to the left of the control booth, the other to the right. We entered the left side first and could either go up some stairs to a second tier of cells or stay on the ground for a stroll along the bottom row. Tony had said he liked to spend time visiting with the inmates. I didn't know if he meant 20 minutes or four hours, and did not ask. He gave me a bunch of cookies and said go upstairs.

"You're not coming with me?" I asked.

"I'm starting downstairs," he said. "Just introduce yourself, ask if they want cookies and shake their hands if they stick them through the bars. (NOTE: This was before the COVID-19 pandemic). Ask how they're doing and they'll start talking. Trust me, they'll want cookies."

At that moment I decided that Tony taught his children how to swim by throwing them in the deep end.

Death row is as foreboding as what I had seen on TV. The floor is concrete and paint is peeling off the walls; the place is dark and smells like a locker room, groin sweat, and a public restroom combined. The cells are different than those I passed earlier — no bars floor to ceiling, just metal doors that slide open and small openings — or "flaps" — with slots for food deliveries and the like.

In all the time I spent there, I never saw an open cell door. At eye level, each door has a square flap that swings out toward the visitor. They are about 18 inches by 18 inches. When open, there are bars separating the visitor from the inmate. Most of the inmates stood close to the opening with arms resting between the bars or on top of the food tray slot.

The only thing on the outside of each cell is a notecard with the inmate's name, date of birth, and race. As I approached each cell, the inmate would say, "Hey Steve," which caught me by surprise initially. I had forgotten that I was wearing a nametag. I spent three hours that first day in what most people would consider Hell on Earth. I spoke with 34 of the 37 residents, and I shook most of their hands.

I was told inmate James' flap remained shut because, "He's not all there." He never wears clothes, spits out most of his food, and smears his own feces on the floor and walls. I spoke to him briefly through the door, but couldn't shake his hand because the flap remained closed, thank goodness. He's 46 years old and convicted of shooting at students and teachers at an elementary school in Greenwood in 1988. Two eight-year-old girls were killed. He had been on death row for 26 years, serving 175 years plus his death sentence.

There were other visits with death row residents especially memorable that day:

— Big Johnny used a screwdriver to stab a man to death more than 60 times in his head, neck, and back. Big Johnny is 6'5" and 280 pounds. He is serving 35 years plus his death sentence. He seemed to be a nice, calm, appreciative guy. He was not fat, but he does put substantially more pressure on Earth's surface than most human beings. If you've seen the movie *The Green Mile*, Big Johnny would be John Coffey. He wanted to make sure I didn't skip the guy next to him whose name is also John.

— John, a cop killer, was in a lot of pain that day because he was undergoing chemotherapy. He said he hopes the state kills him before the cancer does.

 — Steven Bixby was shirtless and certainly did not smell like a bouquet of roses. As soon as I walked up to his cell, he complimented me on my first name. Steven is in for fatally shooting two Abbeville police officers in an attempt to stop the State Department of Transportation from widening a road on his land. He proclaimed his innocence repeatedly. I listened, gave him cookies, shook his hand, and moved on.

— Richard killed a clerk while robbing a convenience store. He's serving 45 years in addition to his death sentence. He's been on the row for 15 years. I spent more time talking with Richard than anyone else that day. Like me, he is from Michigan. Our conversation topics included homemade cookies and Michigan football. We talked about athletes Jim Harbaugh, Derek Jeter, and T.J. Duckett as well as movie star Marilyn Monroe. I asked him if he gets to go outside.

Death row inmates have access to what they call "dog runs" — cages enclosed on the sides. Richard said each of them is supposed to get an hour out there daily, which seldom happens. He said he spends 23 hours and 40 minutes of nearly every day in his cell. The other 20 minutes is in the shower. I asked him if he talks to his neighbors, even though he can't see them. He said that he did.

"That's all I got man. I get along with everyone in here except one guy. Everyone's pretty chill. We're all in the same boat."

I asked which inmate he didn't get along with and he pointed across the tier. "Right over there on the corner. You'll see why when you get there."

Richard asked me why I was sweating so much. I had on a red, dri-fit polo shirt, and my perspiration was showing through.

"Because it's hot as hell in here and I'm very nervous," I said.

"Gotcha," he smiled and said.

Before I left, Richard reached through the bars to shake my hand. I gave him my hand and he held it for probably 10 seconds. "Thank you, Steve. When are you coming back?"

I told him I didn't know then headed straight to the corner cell. I wondered why Richard didn't like the man who lived here. Upon arrival, he opened his flap and I noticed a red-and-white Ohio State University sticker on the inside of it. As he opened it, Richard yelled: "GO BLUE! Now you know why I don't like him!"

The three of us laughed about the rivalry between the state universities. I thought to myself, here I am in a hellhole among the worst criminals in the state — cop killers, people who murder children, rapists — yet they still have a sense of humor.

— Jonathan, aka Jamie, is on the row for killing a woman he did not know. He broke into her home, waited six hours for her to arrive, then shot her in the abdomen. His criminal history also includes a conviction for first-degree criminal sexual conduct with a minor — his infant daughter. He told an investigator that he was curious to know if an infant could be sexually aroused — which is tough to read, I know. I stopped at his cell, looked and was shocked. He looked like a woman with long black hair.

"Hi Steve, call me Jamie," he said.

I looked beyond him as I did with the other inmates to see what was in his cell. What appeared to be a bra was hanging from his bunk. For some reason, I extended my right hand to shake his.

"No, left hand only, Steve," he said. "I've seen you shake all these guy's hands and I know what they do with their right hand."

His death sentence has since been overturned. He is currently serving 30 years on the charge of criminal sexual conduct with a minor along with a life sentence for first-degree burglary.

— Stephen Stanko sat in the next cell. I remembered his case in the news. A large Gamecocks sticker was on a wall in his cell, so I asked if he was a fan.

"Yes. I have degrees from the University of South Carolina, and I've published several books," he said.

We talked about his education in addition to Gamecocks football. He killed his live-in girlfriend, raped her 15-year-old daughter, and slit her throat, and later killed a 74-year-old man and stole his vehicle. Stanko is serving 130 years in addition to the death penalty.

— My final visit that first day was with a man named Clinton, who seemed generally happy, saying he was having a great day. He had been on death row for 13 years for killing his four-month-old daughter. He shook, squeezed, slapped, punched, bit, and strangled his child before breaking her back on a crib rail because she wouldn't stop crying. He begged the jury for the death penalty, saying he deserved to die.

I didn't know the specifics of the crimes of each of those men until after I left that day. The inmates seemed somewhat ordinary and they carried on relatively normal conversations. Each of their cells had a steel bunk bed, a toilet, a chair, and a small desk. The interior designs varied. Some were cozier than others. Each man had a green coverall suit hanging somewhere in the cell. Green is the color designated to death row inmates for some reason.

Most had small television sets that cost $250, I was told. I asked Clinton how many channels he received. He said 16, adding the guys on the back wall got 18 because service was better over there. The grass always seems greener.

I was surprised to see a library on death row. It's a vacant cell filled with books wall to wall, ceiling to floor. Each inmate is allowed to check out four books at once. The librarian stops in every three months.

As we were leaving, I heard a lot of yelling in there. I asked Tony what was going on. He said several inmates play chess with each other by yelling out their moves. It was rather strange because death row is typically quiet, dark, and foreboding. We returned to the chapel and still had about two more hours until it was time to leave. I was exhausted. Shortly after I sat back down with my group, Ron asked where I had been.

"I thought you freaked out and left."

I have no recollection of what else we talked about in the chapel that day. My mind was stuck on the row — on all those men sitting around waiting to die.

Chapter 2

I was speechless after Ron and I got back in my car that September evening. I had been without my cell phone for almost 12 hours. I looked at the screen and noticed several text messages and missed calls. My family and a few friends knew where I was headed that day and were checking on me.

Meanwhile, Ron asked what I thought of my visit. I don't remember what I said. But it didn't matter much. He had visited death row many times before and knew what it was like. It's a 45-minute drive back to Charleston from Lieber. After I dropped off Ron at his house, I thought about those men on the row. Most people don't know very far in advance how they are going to die and where. I had just met 34 who do. I couldn't get the experience out of my mind for many days and nights. I wondered how I would feel if I was in one of those cells awaiting a designated fate. Empathy, not sympathy, I kept reminding myself.

I also wondered what those men do all those days long. I was in there for a few hours and exhausted. The thought of spending the rest of my life like that was a nightmare. How are they treated by the guards? Do family members visit them? Do they have the same rights as inmates in the general population? What do they consider to be a good day? What's a bad one? Did I get an accurate portrayal of what it's like or did they put on a show? Was I tricked into thinking they might be relatively normal people who made a few bad choices?

I compared my visit with death row inmates to scrolling through my Facebook feed and seeing a post from a friend for whom life might seem great even though I knew it was not. People only put on Facebook what they want the world to see and know. Being on social media often makes it seem that people's lives are mostly filled with rainbows and butterflies. That's because portraying nice things about one's own life often enough, even if they are lies, tends to cause others to start to believe them, right?

I also thought about questions that I should have asked those inmates. So I began writing things down — thoughts, reflections, questions — anything pertaining to the experience in case I got a change to return. I also thought about the irony of it: The last place on most people's list of places to visit had suddenly become the first on mine.

I later told Ron how I felt and that I wanted to return. He said the chaplain had already cleared me, and it shouldn't be a problem. Later, during a phone call, the chaplain said I should fill out a Department of Corrections "Application for Volunteer Services" and submit it. So, about a month after my first visit, I filled out the application and gave it to the chaplain along with a copy of my driver's license. The form requested my name, street address, Social Security number, birthdate, place of birth, reason I wanted to volunteer, a criminal history if I had one, whether or not I was on a visitation list for any inmates in South Carolina, if I have any Department of Corrections relationships, my medical needs, emergency contact name and number, and my signature acknowledging that all the information I provided is true.

Six weeks later, I received word that my application was approved. Death row inmates are not allowed direct contact with family members or friends, so before I could return, the authorities needed to make sure I was not related to or had any close relationships with the inmates. All of which made sense to me.

I expected them to tell me to show up for an orientation regarding what I was allowed to do and not do, say and not say. That didn't happen. My only communication with the prison was through the chaplain, who told me to tell the people at the front gate my name and that I was a volunteer.

I admit that ministering to inmates is not what I intended to do. I am not a deeply religious person. I'm not comfortable or confident talking about it with anyone. I can't offer much along those lines other than an occasional "Peace be with you." I wanted to talk to the prisoners about other things.

Ron said the volunteers often pray with the inmates and offer them spiritual advice. He carries a Bible in there with him, which is fine. But I thought it would be good if the inmates had someone to talk to who is not focused on spiritual matters, to visit with someone willing to converse about other things. I figured it would give them a better sense of self-worth.

Was I nervous? Sure. Was I excited about the opportunity to earn their trust, and to learn firsthand what life was like for the most violent, manipulative, remorseless people in South Carolina? Absolutely. I didn't have an agenda. I'm not a reporter working on a news story, and I wasn't an aspiring author doing research on what I hoped would be a blockbuster. I didn't seek to exploit the worst that the human race has to offer. I was simply curious about the prison system and the psychology of killers. I wanted to know who they are, from where they came and if they thought prison was rehabilitating. But, as I've learned from being a teacher and school administrator, you can't put a child in a classroom without a teacher and expect them to learn anything. I wanted to know if killers were capable of changing and if the death penalty deters crime. I was trying to determine how I actually felt about capital punishment.

Once the word got out about my visit, I received a lot of feedback from people in the form of emails, phone calls, text messages, via Facebook, and in person. I told them I was fascinated by the experience, and didn't realize so many others were too. Some shared their own experiences on the wrong side of the law. But most of the responses were things like:

— "That's really cool that you got to do that."

— "I'm also interested in prisons."

— "How did you get permission to get in?"

— "Were you scared?"

— "What's it really like in there?"

I answered all of those easily, but a few people asked tougher ones:

— "Why did you do that?" (with expressions on their faces indicating what they really wanted to ask was, "Why would you want to talk with the worst criminals in the state? They should be locked up and isolated so they can think about their crimes for the rest of their lives.")

One person said my kindness was misplaced, which got me to thinking:

— Was I being kind to them?

— If so, how could it be misplaced?

— Should I direct my kindness to others instead?

— Is kindness ever actually misplaced, or should it be given freely to everyone, everywhere?

Misplaced kindness is a tough one. Some people don't think death row inmates deserve to have visitors. Others do. I think they should as long as the inmate is not so dangerous and/or deranged that he must be separated with an additional chain-link fence as previously noted. However, none of my loved ones were victims of any of those men. If so, I might be one who believes that we should lock 'em up and throw away the keys. I hope I never find out.

I tried to counter a few of the implied criticisms with excuses that included the words "curiosity," "fascination," and "because I'm interested and I care." But mostly I responded with, "I don't really know." I'm working to come up with a better answer because I come from a long line of folks who give a damn about others no matter what.

One reason I wanted to go back was to better understand the impact my visits were having not only on the inmates, but also on me. I think they appreciated — maybe even enjoyed — my first visit. I think they felt that way because death row dwellers have been dehumanized and virtually silenced since their arrests. The public hasn't heard their voices. Their lawyers speak for them. Prosecutors typically try to dehumanize people like them to help convince jurors to agree that they must pay the ultimate price from their crimes. It's easier to order the execution of a monster.

I'm convinced that, if defendants in capital murder cases are allowed to testify on their own behalf, more would be spared the death penalty. I believe this because of what I saw and heard that first day that I visited Lieber. I witnessed the basic humanity of most of those men, and I'm a very good judge of character.

Several people said they wanted to accompany me next time I went. I told them a visit to death row is not like going to a wedding: My invitation didn't come in the mail, and I wasn't allowed to bring a date. I think it would be a good thing if more people were allowed to visit those men. It is important for each of us to realize that condemned men living on South Carolina's death row are condemned in the name of every citizen in the state. If more people understood this fact, there might be fewer — if any — death sentences handed down.

One reason people are fascinated with celebrities is because it's hard to relate to their lifestyles. Most celebrities live their lives attuned to how others perceive them. This affects what a celebrity thinks he or she must have, and where they go in public, who they date, what they wear. All the while, most observers assume celebrities will always have more money and fame than they do. My fascination with death row is like that — but in reverse. I can't relate to a condemned killer's lifestyle, although I've had far more given to me that they ever have. I'm also convinced I won't be stuck in a tiny cell, wearing the same clothes, doing the same things over and over with no hope of getting out.

What would my state of mind be if I were caged like a dog all day for the rest of my life? I could not fully comprehend the horror of it — which is another reason why I wanted to return. I have empathy, not sympathy, for those condemned men.

I was not fully prepared for what I experienced that first day. I didn't know I would spend three hours inside a building with 37 condemned men. As I said earlier, one of my first impressions of death row was that it is eerily quiet. I was also very nervous and concentrated more on controlling my bowels than asking well-considered questions.

Those men are facing the harshest punishment a person can receive as designated under US law. The "state" ordered them sent to an early grave. And the "state" has done this in your name and my name and in every other citizen's name. Most of us don't fully understand this, which is a shame.

I decided that the next time I arrived in the parking lot at Lieber, I would be better prepared. As I said, one of my original goals was to help those inmates benefit to some degree from seeing and talking to me. I don't think they did during my first visit. I was uncomfortable, to say the least, and surely they sensed it. I intended to have meaningful conversations on my return visit. So I was better prepared this time with my questions:

— How would you feel if Dylann Roof — the racist, Charleston AME church killer — became your next-door neighbor? Would you want to beat the crap out of him? Would that even be possible on death row?

— Do you, a condemned man, approve of capital punishment?

— Do you believe in your heart of hearts that you belong on death row?

— Do you keep up with anyone on the outside? Do you still have friends and a family? If so, what do they think of you now?

— Why do you have what seems to be a better sense of optimism than most inmates in the general prison population? The last time I was here, I noticed that some, if not most, of you on death row smile a lot.

— What's the best way to reduce violence on the outside? Do you hate cops? If so, why? How can we change that perception? Smart people have big ideas on what should be done to reduce violence and change perceptions about police officers but apparently no one has asked people like you, who have firsthand knowledge of these things that should be done. Am I correct?

My second trip to death row was January 9, 2017, and indeed I was better prepared. I was confident that I could tell the difference between inmates who seemed to enjoy my company more than the sugar in the cookies, so I didn't plan to waste time passing out sweets. I knew the questions I wanted to ask. And, as if I were on my first day in fourth grade, I had already selected clothes to wear: my favorite black T-shirt with "Death Row Records" printed in red and a picture of a guy strapped in an electric chair. But I soon reconsidered. I didn't want to make a fashion statement. I opted for a standard T-shirt instead.

Ron and I arrived at Lieber at 1:30 p.m. on a Monday. In the lobby I saw a big whiteboard noting the number of inmates in various sections of the prison — a total of 1,239 that day. There was a little excitement as we went through security. Ron's body was full of lead and it sounded like a checkout lane at Publix when the wand was passed over him. Next stop was the chaplain's office to sign in. We chatted with the chaplain for a while then proceeded, minus the cookies, to the row. Again, I received no guidance about what was expected of me.

As we crossed the prison yard I noticed an inmate who did not want to return to his dorm and was putting up stiff resistance. An officer directed us away from the disturbance. I wondered what I was supposed to do if things got out of hand. What if an emergency alarm went off? Should I drop to the ground or just stand there like a deer in headlights? Would I run around in circles hoping I don't become a statistic? Stop, drop, and roll maybe?

To get from the chapel to the death row cells, we cleared the seven gates and doors, all of which required someone to buzz us in or physically unlock the barriers. I wasn't as nervous as I was the first time until I reached the long, white-walled hallway in the maximum-security building. Suddenly my stomach sank. My heart pounded as I turned left just before the kitchen and saw the red Death Row sign. The thick steel gate opened, the guards took my keys and everything else in my pockets. I stood facing the wall as they patted me down. Next I had to decide if I wanted to go to the right or left side of the cellblock.

That's when I noticed safety vests hanging on a wall in the lobby: Welcome to our home! Can I interest you in a stab-proof vest before you come in? There was no welcome mat, just the vests. Southern hospitality at its worst.

Death row has a peculiar aroma and it is generally quiet, the combination of which softly stinks. There's a large whiteboard with the inmates' names and addresses on top of a file cabinet. This time I went to the right side first. I wanted to talk with four or five of the men in more depth.

The first was Richard Moore, the guy from Michigan I mentioned earlier. The following was posted on October 23, 2001, on the Spartanburg news site goupstate.com:

During the guilt phase of the trial, prosecutors persuaded the jury that Moore had confronted (the store clerk) with the intent to rob Nikki's. (The clerk) produced a .45-caliber handgun, but Moore overpowered the smaller store clerk and took it from him. Moore then shot at Pacolet resident (name redacted), the only customer inside Nikki's, as (name redacted) played video poker. That gave (the clerk) time to grab another gun and shoot Moore in the left arm. Moore then fired a bullet from the .45 into (the clerk's) left side. It exited through his heart, killing him.

DNA evidence indicated that a profusely bleeding Moore left a blood trail inside Nikki's after the shooting, as he went from place to place in an apparent search for cash. After dripping blood on (the clerk's) body while twice stepping over it, Moore left the small store in Spartanburg County's Whitney community with $1,408 in cash. He drove to a nearby residence, where he tried to buy crack cocaine.

When I got to his cell, Richard was sitting on his bed eating lunch.

"Hey man, how you doing?" I said. "Sorry I interrupted your lunch. I'll come back in a little bit."

"No, no, no. It can wait," Richard said as he hopped off his bed and came to the food flap. "It's just some nasty beef stew or something."

"Do you remember me?" I asked.

Richard: "Yeah man. You the principal from Michigan, ain't you? I didn't think you was ever going to come back. How you been man?"

We shared some small talk before I said I'd like to ask him a couple of personal questions.

Richard: "Sure. Anything."

"Dylann Roof. You're familiar with him, right?"

Richard: "Yes, sir."

"He might be moved into your neighborhood sometime soon. What do you think about that, and what will life be like if he is placed in the cell next to you?"

Richard: "He won't have any problems with me. I got my own demons to deal with. I'm trying to get right with the Lord myself. I ain't got time to worry about his demons."

"Ain't nobody got time for that," I said, forgetting that Richard didn't have access to the Internet so he didn't get my reference to Kimberly "Sweet Brown" Wilkins' comments when asked about escaping her apartment house fire on a YouTube video that went viral.

Richard: "That's right, nobody got time for other people's demons."

It's refreshing to talk to folks who don't have the Internet or know social media. They don't speak in hashtags and there aren't any #TBT ("Throwback Thursdays") on death row; most days don't mean much. Nobody there said, "I know, right?" And even though the struggle is as real as it will ever get, none of them used the phrase, "The struggle is real." Being on the row is like going to your cell phone settings and putting your entire life in airplane mode. I pondered that for a moment: If social media was available to them, trending hashtags might be #LivingMyWorstLife, #WasTodayReallyNecessary?, #GroundhogDay and #BarsForDays.

"You are in arguably the most violent prison in this state. You are segregated with 36 other guys on death row where you await your fate. Are you one of the 37 most violent and dangerous human beings in South Carolina?" I asked.

Richard looked at me for about three seconds and smiled: "No way man. Not even close. The most dangerous people in this state are not in prison. They're out on the street killing people. I made a mistake, but my crime was robbery."

He was right about not being a threat to anyone. He's in prison, and society is somewhat safer, I suppose. But I found it interesting that he had justified his crime, if only to himself. I think it's natural that men on the row might justify what they've done. None more so than Steven Bixby, who is serving 65 years on top of two death sentences. The following was taken from the Greenwood newspaper site indexjournal.com, posted on April 22, 2018:

Abbeville County deputy Danny Wilson left the South Carolina Department of Transportation Office at about 8:40 a.m. on Dec. 8, 2003 to head to Union Church Road. The Bixby family, who lived on the road, had been interfering with survey work for the widening of S.C. Highway 72 — screaming profanities at workers, making threats and pulling up survey stakes, and throwing them into the middle of the road. The highway department planned to use an easement the previous owner of the land had granted to widen the road, which enraged the Bixbys.

The family moved to Abbeville from Warren, N.H. in the 1990s. When S.C. Department of Transportation officials tried to show Rita Bixby proof of the easement, she dismissed them as lies and forgeries. Fearful for the safety of their workers and hindered by the Bixbys' regular interference, highway officials contacted police. Wilson went to the house after meeting with DOT about the matter. As he approached the house, Steven Bixby shot him, dragged him inside and handcuffed him. Wilson's cruiser remained idling outside. Law enforcement was not aware of what happened to Wilson, but after not hearing from him and receiving reports of a running police car outside the house, officers began to arrive.

Deputy Deborah Graham and State Constable Donnie Ouzts tried to find Wilson. The two approached the house then waited for backup. As they walked away from the house, Steven Bixby shot Ouzts in the back, killing him. Graham, who was standing near Ouzts when he was killed, testified in 2007. "It had to be his back because both of us had turned to walk away," she said. "I saw him fall."

After Ouzts was shot, hundreds of law enforcement officers from across the state surrounded the house and a 13-hour standoff ensued. At 7:15 p.m., an armored personnel carrier was sent in to knock down a door, power to the outside lights around the house was cut off and a robot was sent inside. An hour later, officers used a vehicle to remove a trailer near the house. In the process, a propane tank near the house caught fire and emergency personnel extinguished the blaze.

Between 8:50 and 9:20 p.m., Steven Bixby and his father, Arthur, exchanged gunfire with law enforcement, and police officers deployed tear gas into the house. Arthur Bixby, who had been wounded in the exchange, turned himself into authorities sometime after 10 p.m. Steven Bixby surrendered himself shortly afterward.

Steven Bixby's cell is covered with his writings, mostly about Trump and police officers. He's a Trump supporter who hates all cops. He made that clear. On the door of his cell, a note says: "Please send all future Father's Day cards to: Donald Trump, 1700 Pennsylvania Avenue, Washington, D.C. Trump is our Daddy." As I read it, Bixby stood up from his bed and walked over to me.

"Hey," I said, "I was just reading your sign about future Father's Day cards and I couldn't help but notice that you have the address wrong for the White House. It's 1600 Pennsylvania Ave., not 1700."

Bixby: "I did that on purpose. I changed the 16 to 17 to represent the 17 candidates he beat out for the presidency."

I asked him about a sign in his cell that said, "Police lives don't matter. They only care about themselves, and they're ALL CORRUPT!"

"Surely you don't believe they're all corrupt, do you?" I said.

Bixby: "Every single one of them. If they're not personally corrupt, they're indirectly corrupt. They all cover up for each other."

Talking to Bixby was like talking to an over-the-top vegan, cross-fitter, or long-distance runner. All he wanted to talk about was his own case, saying there was a difference between murder and just killing someone, and that what he did was not murder.

"So what did you do?"

Bixby: "I called the police and told them not to send another cop to my property. I warned them. They sent one anyway. When he came, he got shot. We took him inside the house, put his handcuffs on him, and read him his Miranda rights. We did a citizen's arrest. When they couldn't get in touch with that officer, they sent a backup. When that officer arrived at my house, he was shot and died on my front lawn."

I mustered the strength to say, "That sounds like murder to me, Mr. Bixby."

Bixby: "Nope. That's a justifiable killing. Big difference."

I asked him about Dylann Roof. Bixby said Roof would get

along just fine on the row. "He'd make friends, no problem. Half the people in here think the same way he does."

As I was wrapping up the conversation, I heard another inmate yelling to a nearby officer: "CO! CO! Come over here!"

The officer yelled back at him, "Settle down, tough guy!"

Bixby: "That's the problem. They have alligator mouths and tadpole asses. They'd never talk to us like that if we weren't locked in here 24/7. They'd be dead in 45 seconds."

All the prisoners I talked with that day told me how inhumane it is living on the row. Note that this was on a Monday, and, they claimed, no one had been out of their cells since Thursday. No shower or dog run or anything. I estimate each cell is only about 12 feet x 7 feet. They said they had not been allowed out in three days.

"You're supposed to get 30 minutes of outdoor time every day," I said to one of the men.

"I haven't been outside in over a month," he said.

Bixby: "This is not a prison in here. Death row is an insane asylum. Out there is a prison, but not here. I don't know how much more of this (expletive) I can take."

Steven Bixby doesn't think he's crazy. He reminded me of Dylann Roof, who said he had to kill all those people in the basement of the Charleston AME church, and he probably still feels that way. Roof doesn't think he's crazy either — exactly the type of person who should be locked up.

Big Johnny and another man who I refer to as the "Chemo Guy" are in adjacent cells. Big Johnny is the one who looks like John Coffey from *The Green Mile* movie — huge and physically imposing. He stabbed a man to death using a screwdriver because the victim owed him money. If I owed Big Johnny money, I'd pay him back fast, with interest. Big Johnny has been on death row for 21 years.

Next door was Chemo Guy, who is older with gray hair. He said he had cancer and claimed that his doctors have his medicine all wrong.

I stood between their cells as I conversed with them. They could see me, but could not see each other. I asked why they seemed more optimistic than inmates I had encountered earlier in the general prison population. "Why do you guys seem to smile more? That's odd to me."

"There are a ton of killers like me on that yard," Chemo Guy said. "They should be grateful. They have no idea what it could be like. I'm just trying to live my dash the best I can."

"Your dash?" I asked.

Chemo Guy: "On your grave will be the year you were born and the year you died. In between is a dash. That's your life. I'm just trying to live my dash the best I can."

He said death row inmates do not have it easy. "If the row was like what you see on TV, it would be heaven for us. People think we shower every day, shoot the (expletive) with each other, play cards, exercise, go outside. It ain't even close to that ... I can't wait to get to Hell, if that's where I'm going."

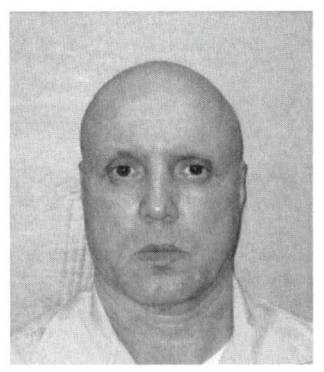

I also spoke with John Weik that day. He seemed to be almost as crazy as Bixby. Weik used a shotgun to murder his former girlfriend while her two children hid in the bathroom. I walked up to his cell and he immediately started talking, and talking, and talking.

"Hey Steve, my last name is Weik.

It has two vowels, back-to-back, but the first one's silent. It's pronounced 'Why-k'. I like to do a lot of origami (Japanese art of paper folding). I don't see a lot of colors in here, so when I get my hands on magazines, I keep them and hang them up. I scraped all the paint off my ceiling and used the paint chips as outer coating for my origami. All you see is garbage, but I see beautiful colors. I have a list of all the people who have been executed in this prison. Do you want to see it? I'm the official list-keeper." His words sounded rehearsed, as if that's his go-to opening line when someone he's never seen before walks up to his cell.

He walked over to his desk, grabbed the list, and walked back. On and on he went.

"Alrighty-then, 'Why-k', I gotta run," I said. "We'll catch up next time."

NOTE: Weik's death sentence has since been overturned. He is now serving two life sentences for murder and first-degree burglary. He no longer lives on death row, which I suppose, is good reason some of the others might be a little more optimistic about their own fates.

I spent most of my time on death row that day with Stephen Stanko — about 45 minutes. He killed his girlfriend, raped her 15-year-old daughter, slit her throat, left her for dead, then killed a 74-year-old man before stealing his car. The television news shows *Dateline* and *48 Hours* covered the story.

Stanko is extremely intelligent — maybe schizophrenic or bipolar or something similar. He has authored some books, most of them while in prison. He said college professors write asking him to call them on certain days and times. Stanko claims that, when he calls them from his cell (his living quarters, not his cell phone), his voice is projected into an auditorium full of students, and he "basically conducts the class." He said he is a sought-after author in the field of prisoner psychology. If true, it's a subject about which he should know a lot. In addition to his death sentence, Stanko is serving 130 years for two counts of armed robbery, assault and battery with intent to kill, criminal sexual conduct, and kidnapping.

I asked about his books. He went to his desk, picked up a book and walked back to show it to me, which would've added somewhere around eight steps to your daily Fitbit step counter. His name was at the bottom of the cover: "Stephen Stanko, Independent Researcher." I asked him why it says independent researcher and not death row inmate.

Stanko: "Some of the contributing authors refused to allow their names next to a death row inmate, so they made me take that off. They have huge egos."

I peppered him with more questions and his responses seemed honest. I had heard that Stanko has an IQ of 143, which is close to genius. He asked where I worked. After I told him, he said, "Great school. My favorite teacher was a part-time guidance counselor there."

About 20 minutes into our conversation, he said, "I enjoy talking to you, Steve. Most of my visits go the exact same way. They walk by my cell, look up at my name, their jaws drop because they remember my case or have seen *Dateline*. They say hello and keep walking."

"Did my jaw drop when I saw your name?" I asked.

Stanko: "Yes, it did, but you stopped and asked a lot of good questions. I don't get intelligent conversations very much in here. It's been a long time, actually."

After that, a guard walked by his cell. "Excuse me," Stanko said, looking directly at the guard. In a slightly elevated, stern tone he said, "Tell your sarge I want my shower!"

Guard: "My sarge isn't here."

Stanko: "Well then, go tell the warden that I want my shower. Tell him Stanko wants his shower right now!"

The guard walked away. Stanko looked at me and returned to his monotone voice: "Sorry about that. I haven't had a shower since Thursday."

"No problem," I thought. "I haven't had a morsel of food in two hours and I'm about to eat my finger. I feel your pain."

Stanko: "Why do you come here — to death row?"

"I'd like to think I'm having an impact on you; that you benefit from it," I said, "but I feel like I take more away from this than y'all do."

Stanko: "Don't underestimate yourself. Most of the guys in here don't have anybody, anything, any hope or any dreams. You have to have a dream if you're going to have a dream come true. I try to tell them that, but most don't get it. Freddie down there tried to stab a guard last month, so don't get too comfortable with anyone in here. That's just Freddie being Freddie, but the point I'm trying to make is be careful in here."

Freddie was in a cell fenced off from the row — isolated from the most isolated prisoners in the state's most isolated prison unit. You don't need to be Kris Kringle to know who's been naughty or nice on death row. Although Freddie and others were fenced off, they could still get cookies from the visitors. The fence protected the visitor, or prison staff, from getting close enough to Freddie for him to harm them. Prisoners are crafty, though. I witnessed Tony give a fenced off prisoner his cookies by placing the bag of delicious wafers onto a broom, which the prisoner extended through the bars of his cell.

Stanko continued: "It's important that you say hello to everyone in here because this is everything to most of us. You're doing a good thing and God notices. When you come back, I'll have some things for you to read that I think you'll be interested in. What you need to do now is start journaling. Write your thoughts down."

Here I was, hanging on every word this death row inmate was

saying. He made a lot of sense. It was tough talking to those men without having their crimes lingering in my head. But I did listen intently and valued what they said. I also took a lot of notes.

I've never been a firm believer in capital punishment, but I haven't had strong feelings of opposition either. I believe in second chances. I believe that good people are capable of doing bad things, and I believe in rehabilitation. My background in education has much to do with how I feel.

I think some people have committed such awful crimes that they belong behind bars, maybe for life. But after my second visit to Lieber I was thinking that executing them seems immoral if not unconstitutional. I'm going to say this again because I think it's that important: The state is killing them in the name of all South Carolinians. Most of us don't fully understand that.

Capital punishment is not legal in every state. It is in South Carolina, although the state hasn't executed anyone since 2011, primarily because authorities can't get chemicals used for lethal injections. In South Carolina, the name of a company that does provide chemicals is considered public information. For the owners, managers, and even the employees of the company, the matter becomes both a moral and business dilemma.

South Carolina's death row inmates can choose the method by which they are executed: lethal injection or electrocution. Surely their lawyers advise them to choose lethal injection because the deadly chemical cocktail is so hard to obtain.

It's also interesting to note that more than 150 death row inmates nationwide have been exonerated since 1976, the year the penalty was reinstated in the United States. In that same amount of time, states have executed more than 1,400 people. That means for every 10 people executed in this country since the death penalty was reinstated, at least one has been exonerated for the basic charge that landed all of them on death row. So I'm thinking, if one can of beer is spoiled in every 12-pack the beer truck delivers, stores would stop selling that particular brand, right?

Thus, if statistics actually mean anything, there is a 100 percent chance our judicial system executes people for crimes they did not commit. On top of that, because of all the appeals permitted in death penalty cases, it costs an estimated $1.1 million more in taxpayers' money after someone is sentenced to execution than it does for him or her to receive life in prison. At that point in my reasoning process, I couldn't help recalling popular hip-hop performer Tupac Shakur saying no one has the right to kill another person in his song "Only God Can Judge Me Now." (That's two Death Row Records references that I have made, if you're counting.)

Anyway, after my second visit to the row, I still had questions about incarceration, capital punishment, and rehabilitation:

— Does executing someone deter others from committing crimes?

— Does it solve anything?

— Does it provide closure to victims' families?

— Do those loved ones care that I'm talking with these guys?

On our way home that evening, my conversation with Ron centered on Stanko, who seemed to be very intelligent, so much so that I couldn't picture him doing the heinous things that he did. Unbeknownst to me at that time, Ron knew Stephen Stanko because they had been imprisoned in the same facility. Stanko was serving time for kidnapping and assault while Ron was doing time for his role in the car chase.

When I got back home, I Googled the *48 Hours* and *Dateline* episodes about Stanko, watched both and wrote down questions for our next talk.

Chapter 3

The 30 years preceding the day in 1999 when Ron Burris was shot by police were anything but normal, he said. He was born in Maryland, the youngest of six siblings — four boys and two girls. He was only a year old when his parents divorced. His father was not around during Ron's younger years. His mother worked to support the children.

Ron remembers crying a lot during those times. He knew something wasn't right. He was five years old when he moved to Charleston with his mother, stepfather, two of his brothers, and one of his sisters. His other sister and brother stayed in Maryland with their father.

Ron's stepfather owned a sewing machine business and landed a contract with the local school district to do the maintenance of a variety of machines and appliances. Ron remembers going with him frequently to repair the equipment. At first, he wasn't fond of his stepdad because it seemed as if he was trying to take the place of his real father.

Ron was held back in second grade and promoted socially every year afterward. He can't remember a single time when he felt smart or proud of himself academically. By the time he was in middle school, Ron's mother was sending him back to Maryland in the summers to be with his father and the other siblings. He was 12 years old and his father was teaching him the asphalt trade.

Ron loved being with his dad, and they had a special bond. But his brothers were jealous. They thought Ron was stealing their father's affection. They often beat Ron physically and mentally, he said. He was hurt in ways that he did not want to talk about. They also threatened Ron with even more violence if he told anyone what they were doing to him.

Ron's father drank a lot of beer and smoked a lot of cigarettes at the time. Ron was only 10 years old when he started doing the same. His criminal career began in his middle school years. Stealing was his thing.

Under the apprenticeship of a female thief he viewed as an authority figure, the duo often hit various department stores. She would prep him on what to do and where to stand while she slipped items into her handbag. They were very good at it. They also stole from grocery stores, gas stations, and pretty much anywhere, he said.

Ron soon decided he didn't need her help to get things he wanted, so he became a one-man show. He was in the sixth grade when he slipped into his neighbors' house while they were gone. He knew where they had a safe. He returned home with stolen money, which he showed to his brothers. Soon afterward, the brothers backed their car into the neighbors' driveway, went inside, removed the entire safe, loaded it in their car and returned home. Inside the safe they found expensive jewelry, including a woman's ring.

One of the brothers gave the ring to a girl he was trying to impress. She told her boyfriend, who was not impressed. The boyfriend told his father, who happened to be a police officer.

Ron and his brothers had stashed the safe in some woods behind a school. Police soon found it and the Burris boys were taken in for questioning. Ron was released to the custody of his mother and stepfather. His brothers were charged with burglary and fined. Christmas was canceled that year in the Burris household.

By the time Ron was in ninth grade at James Island High School, he was breaking into cars on a regular basis. He got caught sometimes, but it didn't matter. He didn't like going to school, and when he did he often got into fights. He eventually was charged with assault and battery, fined, and placed on probation. Still, none of that mattered to him. His mother had no control over him, so he did whatever he wanted.

When asked the highest grade he completed, Ron said, "I know

I made it to 10th grade, but I can't say how far along I got."

Ron was 16 years old when he was invited to spend the night at a friend's house. They smoked marijuana and drank liquor until his friend passed out. Ron was about to do the same when his friend's mother tapped him on his leg and asked him to come with her into the kitchen.

"She was a good-looking woman, so I got up and went with her," Ron said. When he sat down at the kitchen table, he saw a line of white powder laid out on the table.

"I want you to try it," she said.

Ron obliged. Before that moment, he had been depressed about everything in his life. After that moment, he felt great. He loved cocaine, and basically became a servant for the woman, whose husband worked long hours at the Naval Shipyard in North Charleston.

Ron did her grocery shopping, errands, and whatever she asked him. She gave him cocaine.

She soon asked him to join her on drug runs to the airport, where they picked up men who didn't speak English. He remembers one run in which the man with an accent pulled out a foreign newspaper, unrolled it and introduced Ron to "fish scale cocaine" — the highest quality available.

Ron, 17, soon realized he was working for a Colombian drug cartel. He would drive to the airport, pick up drug runners, take them where they needed to go, and serve as a security guard. Ron later learned from a friend how to freebase cocaine for a more intense high. His friend was later arrested and taken to the booking area at the county jail, where he grabbed a guard's taser and threatened to use it against him. Another guard came in, a fight ensued, and Ron's friend was killed.

Ron quit school altogether and moved in with his friend's mother. Ron's mother objected but he ignored her. He didn't care what she said or thought. By the time he was 18, Ron was on his own and living mostly in Maryland, where he worked with one of his brothers in the asphalt business. Every dollar he earned (and stole) was spent on drugs. Ron was in his 20s when he was imprisoned in both Maryland and South Carolina for burglary and drugs. His specialty was robbing drug dealers.

"I was extremely good at it," Ron said.

Earlier in his life while breaking into cars, Ron had snatched police and security-service badges. Later, he and a buddy would drive into North Charleston neighborhoods where drug sales often occurred. One neighborhood in particular they called the Hot Spot. Ron would drive while his friend rode in the front passenger's seat. They would engage a dealer then ask him to get into the back seat to make a transaction. After the dealer showed them the drugs, Ron would remove a badge and yell, "North Charleston Metro. Don't f---ing move!"

They got the dealer out of the car and started patting him down, Ron said. "If you don't do exactly what the real cops do, the dealers will know you're fake and start shooting, so it's extremely important that you don't break character," he said, adding that he would give the pushers just enough space to run because that's what they always do.

"I played that role so good," Ron said. "No smiling, no nonsense. You can't give them any reason to make them think you're not a cop because you could get killed."

When the dealer took off running, Ron and his buddy followed. "If you don't chase them for a while, they'll know you're not a cop," he said. "Also, you won't get all their dope because they usually empty their pockets as they're running."

These encounters were part of Ron's weekly routine. It was the only way he could get the drugs that he needed. Sometimes he'd have a partner, but many times he would go on his own.

Ron continued to get in trouble, and the court had ordered him to enroll at a drug rehab center in Charlotte. That morning as he sat in the lobby of the place, he decided to bail. He went outside, called a taxi, and went to the city bus station, where he knew homeless people congregated. He needed a fix. The cab pulled up at the station and Ron told the driver to wait for him because he would be right back.

Ron approached some dealers, who asked what he wanted. When the drugs were laid out in front of him to inspect, Ron pulled out his badge and yelled, "Charlotte Metro!"

Everyone ran. Ron scooped up the drugs, sprinted back to the taxi, jumped in the back, and hollered "GO!" The driver threatened to call the police.

"I am the (expletive) police. Drive!" Ron said. When he realized that they were headed to the police station, Ron jumped out of the cab and took off. For Ron, it was just another Tuesday.

The day was August 23, 1999. Ron, 31, was out on bond at that time after being charged with three counts of failure to stop for blue lights. Each count had a maximum of five years in prison. "I never stopped for blue lights," he said.

The night before, a drug dealer sold Ron some bad stuff. Ron was angry. He had been out all night driving around in his wife Kim's car. He pulled into the driveway at his house and went inside. Kim was waiting for him. It wasn't the first time her husband had been in trouble. She had bailed him out before under the pretense that he would change his ways. When Ron arrived that night to change clothes, get his police badge, and exchange her car for his truck, Kim started yelling. She said she would call the cops and demand that his bond be revoked.

Meanwhile, Kim's sister arrived and parked her car behind Ron's truck, preventing him from leaving. Kim went outside and slashed a tire on the truck. He was enraged, strung out and dead set on getting that dealer back for ripping him off.

Ron got into his truck, rammed into his sister-in-law's car and knocked down the neighbor's fence. He knew he wouldn't get very far with a slashed tire so he drove to a nearby auto repair shop, parked his truck, and headed across the street to a car dealership. He perused the lot and chose a Ford Crown Victoria that looked like a police car. It had a V-8 engine with dual exhaust. "Something that would run," Ron said.

The car was green and more than capable of getting him to where he needed to go quickly. As the salesman approached, Ron prepared to haggle over the price. He wanted the man to work for the sale, and played the role well.

"Take it for a ride," the salesman insisted. When Ron got behind the wheel he noticed that the car needed fuel. So he told the salesman, who was in the front passenger seat, they needed to get gas. "That's fine," the salesman said, "pull into that station and we'll fill it up."

Ron pulled into an Exxon station. The salesman went inside to pay with a credit card. Ron knew he could only pump a small amount of fuel before the salesman returned. As soon as the pump was turned on, he put some fuel in the tank and took off toward North Charleston, now riding solo. He stopped at a traffic light and a police cruiser pulled up next to him. The cop stared at Ron, who stared back momentarily before he flipped him the finger and drove off.

The officer got behind Ron and flipped on the blue lights. Ron floored the Crown Victoria and left the cruiser in his dust. Upon arriving in North Charleston, he found some dealers in the usual places and obtained a small quantity of drugs. But the dealer Ron wanted was not around. He stopped at another gas station and was pumping more fuel when he noticed a Budweiser beer truck parked in front of the store. The side hatch was left open while the driver was inside arranging the delivery.

Ron finished pumping the gas, grabbed some cases of beer off the truck, and drove back to the place where he bought drugs. He sold the beer cheap there, raised enough cash to buy more drugs and fuel, and headed for James Island to rob some dealers closer to home. Upon arrival at the next hangout, Ron pulled out his badge and approached the dealers, who dropped what they had and ran. Ron collected the discarded contraband, got back into the car, and left. As he drove down the island's main road, he saw a police cruiser parked on the shoulder. Ron pulled up next to the officer and stopped.

"Quit chasing me before someone gets hurt," Ron demanded. "Those drug dealers ripped me off and I'm going to get my money back. You're not taking me alive." Ron noticed that the officer was fumbling for his gun, so he took off. "I wasn't going to get shot in the face."

The sun was up when Ron needed to refuel. He pulled into a gas station and, as he began pumping, a Jeep Cherokee pulled up. He recognized the driver — an undercover officer — who got out of his vehicle, ran toward Ron, pulled out his gun, and yelled "Police! Freeze!"

Ron dropped the gas handle, jumped into the Crown Victoria and slammed the door shut. But the driver-side window was down. The officer reached in and tried to yank the key out of the ignition. A fight ensued and Ron panicked.

With a jolt, he leaned toward the floorboard on the passenger side, pretending to reach for a gun that he did not have. The officer shot Ron in the stomach. The bullet entered through his abdomen and exited near his groin. Wounded and bleeding profusely, Ron put the car in gear before being shot again, this time in the back. As he drove away, he heard the officer yelling into his radio microphone: "Shots fired! Shots fired!"

Ron had lost a lot of blood when he pulled back onto the main road, but he refused to surrender. He said he had a vague concept of God at that point in his life and told Him he did not want to go to Hell or to prison. Ron kept on driving while asking God for forgiveness. He confessed as many of his sins as he could remember in preparation for his death. He saw no way out of this particular mess, he said, adding that suicide was out of the question.

"People who commit suicide go to Hell," he told me. "But if I piss off enough cops, they'd kill me. So I prayed they'd put me out of my misery."

Driving in broad daylight over the Ashley River bridge from North Charleston, Ron changed his mind about suicide. It was about 2:45 p.m. on a school day and he was in the 231st mile of his 232-mile chase that day. He sped past buses full of children on the way home from school and was extremely upset with God, himself, and everyone in general.

"Why should I care about anyone? Nobody cared about me!" he recalled thinking as he sped through a busy intersection. Ron then cut the wheel sharply in a failed attempt to flip the car. The vehicle left the highway and skidded to a stop in some grass in front of a church. Police cars soon hemmed him on all sides. He was wearing his seatbelt and unscathed except for the bullet wounds. Buckling up was the only thing legal he did that day.

Although surrounded, Ron tried to drive away. The police officers opened fire. Forty-eight rounds were fired at him that day, and 12 of them found their mark. Ron was taken to the hospital, where he spent the next five days in intensive care. Afterward, he was taken to the county jail and arraigned on 11 charges:

— 1 count of assault and battery with intent to kill.

— 3 counts of assault with intent to kill.

— 1 count of assault while resisting arrest.

— 3 counts of resisting arrest with a deadly weapon.

— 2 counts of failure to stop for blue lights.

— 1 count of grand larceny.

The deadly weapon was the green, stolen Crown Victoria. Ron did not own or possess a gun. He appeared before the judge while lying on a stretcher. He faced more than 100 years in prison, and his bond was set at more than $400,000. There was no way he could raise that much money.

Ron was out on bond at that time on a previous charge of failure to stop for blue lights. Six months after the chase, he was in court for the initial charges, and was sentenced to nine years in prison.

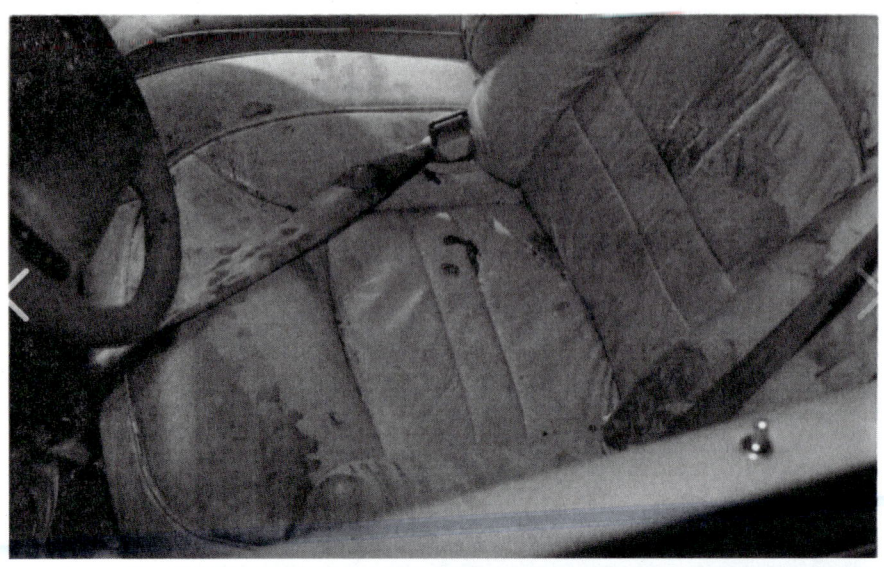

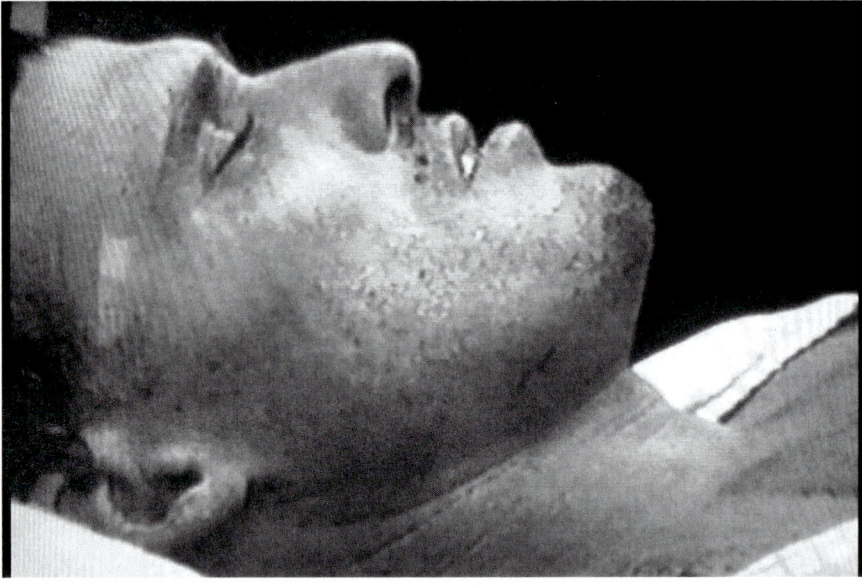

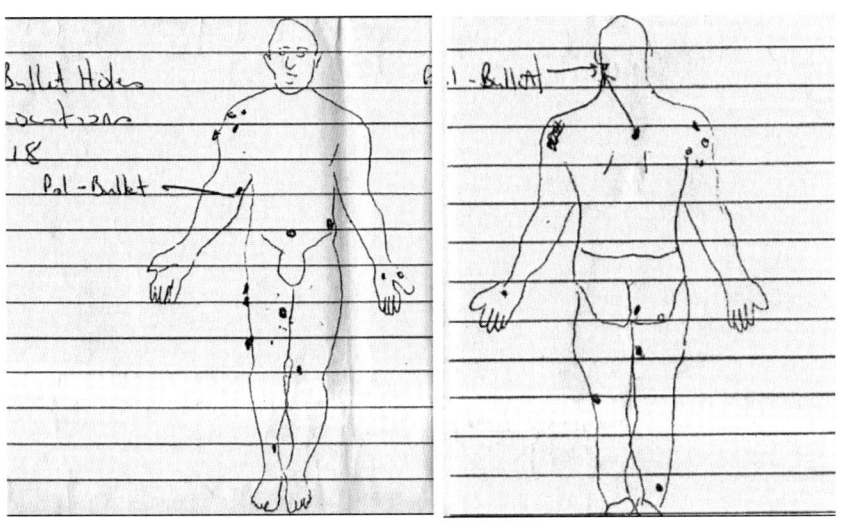

Chapter 4

After the sentencing, Ron was taken to Columbia to await his prison assignment. From there he went to Lieber — the same place I visited 16 years later.

Ron's bus ride from Columbia to Ridgeville took a little over an hour. But he was in no hurry. As far as he was concerned he was en route to Hell. When the bus arrived inside the compound, Ron and the other eight prisoners — all chained together — exited the vehicle and stood against a wall. Their wrists and ankles were shackled. The guards gave Ron a pat-down first, then strip-searched him. After getting a haircut, he was placed in a holding cell with the others and waited to be housed.

It was relatively quiet in the holding cell. The inmates said nothing, made no eye contact. They just sat and waited. Ron did not know what would happen next. Eventually the guards issued Ron and the others their jail clothing, and each was asked a series of questions. Do you have any relatives in this prison? Do you have any enemies? Are you affiliated with any gangs?

Ron answered "no" to all of them while thinking about all the drug dealers he had robbed through the years and how many were imprisoned at Lieber. He was given an identification number and a housing assignment. He was no longer Ron Burris in the eyes of the state. He was prisoner 264243 EA35. His dorm was Edisto A, and 35 was his cell number. He was assigned two "cellies" (roommates), and all three shared a cell intended for two people. Ron slept on a cot. One snored so loudly that Ron could not sleep. He asked to be moved and was denied.

Prisoners often live with numerous unwritten rules and under questionable circumstances. Inmate hierarchy is based on individual crimes. Those who have hurt women or children typically do not have an easy time. Child molesters are often targeted for harm. Rapists too. Ron's crime — against police — typically garners respect from other inmates. This is what is known as "street cred."

A significant number of locals are lodged in Lieber because of its close proximity to Charleston. Many of the inmates knew about Ron's case. He was spared violence and threats of violence. Although he got along with his cellies, he didn't spend a lot of time with them. He preferred to hang out "on the rock" watching TV, and attended church services as well. The rock is the common area of a large cellblock.

"You never forget the sound of keys rattling in the morning as the guards walk around unlocking the cells for chow time," Ron said. "And you never forget to courtesy flush the toilet ... you drop one and flush." That's an unwritten rule. "Nobody wants to smell another man's filth. I still do the courtesy flush to this day."

Ron was not at Lieber long when he was awakened by screams in the middle of the night of a man in a nearby cell. The man, a recent arrival, was fighting for his life. Everyone was locked in for the night, and it was too late by the time the guards arrived. The young man was raped by his older cellmate and bleeding badly. He was removed from the cell, and the next morning life in Edisto A resumed like nothing had happened. Ron never saw the young man again and has no idea what happened to him.

Meanwhile in Charleston, one of Ron's brothers — a firefighter — had a problem. He was a recreational drug user and the department had increased testing of personnel. Driving home one evening, his brother had a minor car accident not far from his home. The driver of the other car called the police. His brother told the other driver he needed to go home to get his insurance information and would be right back.

But Ron's brother never came back. He went home and killed himself. Ron was in prison and unable to attend the funeral.

From February 2000 until March 2001, Ron was at Lieber while preparing for his trial. His lawyer advised him to plead guilty to assault with intent to kill and assault with a deadly weapon in order to avoid a long prison sentence. Ron declined. "I didn't assault or try to kill anyone. I'm not pleading to that. No way!"

So, Ron stood trial on all the charges. All but a few witnesses who were called to testify were police officers who had participated in the chase. Some of their statements were true, Ron said, but others were not.

"Two of the officers got up there and testified that I turned the car at them and tried to hit them. That never happened. I had plenty of opportunities to hit them if that's what I wanted to do. I didn't want to hurt them. I wanted to hurt the drug dealer who ripped me off," Ron said. "I did steal a car and had no intentions of returning it. I did run from the police. I did resist arrest. Those are the things I did. I admit to that, but I would not admit to anything I didn't do."

Against the advice of his attorney, Ron took the stand and told the jury he was guilty of some of the charges but that he did not try to kill anyone that day. The officer who Ron told to quit chasing him testified that Ron issued no threat. Actually he was rather polite, the officer testified. The woman from the store where Ron stole the beer testified that he didn't threaten her either — just took the beer and left.

After three days of trial, the jury got the case and deliberated for nearly 12 hours. Ron and his attorney were optimistic because, typically, the longer the jury is out, the more favorable the outcome for the defendant.

Ron was found guilty of grand larceny, failure to stop for blue lights, resisting arrest, assault while resisting arrest and resisting arrest with a deadly weapon (the car). The jury was hung on the more serious charges of assault with intent to kill, and a mistrial was declared. The judge sentenced him immediately to seven years in prison, running concurrently with the nine years he was already serving. The state would have to decide whether it would drop those charges or try him again.

Ron waited for two days in the county jail before being returned to Lieber. Soon after he was back inside Edisto A, inmates encouraged him to sue the North Charleston Police Department for violating his civil rights. Ron opted to count his blessings instead. But when his mother urged him to sue, Ron changed his mind. Mothers know best, right?

Shortly after Ron did so, an inmate asked if he was familiar with the Bible story about the unforgiving servant. Ron looked it up in the Gospel of Matthew:

Peter asked Jesus how many times his brother could sin against him before he would withhold his forgiveness. Jesus told Peter a story about a king who wanted to settle all debts owed to him by his servants. One told the king he could not pay his debt, and the king ordered that the man, his wife, and their children be sold to cover the bill. The servant begged for patience and promised to repay. The compassionate king forgave the debt, but the servant went to a fellow servant who owed him money, grabbed him by the throat and demanded to be paid in full. The debtor said he could not pay and begged for forgiveness. The first servant refused and had the man thrown into debtors' prison.

The king called the first servant back and asked him why, especially since the king had forgiven the man's debt. The king ordered the first servant to be punished until his debt was paid. Jesus ends the story saying, "So my heavenly Father will also do to you, if you don't forgive your brother from your heart for his misdeeds."

Ron took this passage to heart, especially regarding the mercy shown him by the judge and jury. "How could I turn around and sue the department now?" he asked himself. He also knew the two most serious charges against him had resulted in a mistrial, which meant he might have to return to court. So he wrote the judge: "You showed me a lot of mercy and I will not be an unforgiving servant. I officially withdraw my lawsuit."

But all did not go so well when Ron was at Lieber. A guard came to his cell one day and said he was wanted in the office of the associate warden. Upon arrival, the associate warden had on his desk a box of books addressed to Ron.

"This came for you, but you can't have it," was the associate warden's response, according to Ron, who asked him why, saying the books were Christian-themed and sent by his wife. He was told the books were contraband. Ron said he asked that the books be returned to his wife, but was denied. Ron threatened to call his lawyer.

Ron thinks this confrontation was a reason he was soon placed in solitary confinement, where he again had thoughts about suicide. He said he overcame them by focusing on his wife and family. After three days he was returned to his cell in Edisto A.

Lieber is a level 3, maximum-security facility. Ron said that, due to his good behavior, his classification was lowered to level 2, and he was transferred to the Kershaw Correctional Institution near Camden, more than 100 miles away from Charleston. Kershaw had a bad reputation for violence, which included numerous stabbings and other forms of bloodshed. There was a lot of gang activity inside the Kershaw prison too, even more so than at Lieber.

Ron's living situation at Kershaw was the same — two cellies and a cot. He said he was a model inmate, although it wasn't easy. He was not well known there and not as respected as he had been at Lieber. Eventually his classification was lowered to level 1, and he was transferred to the MacDougall Correctional Institution, a minimum-security prison in Ridgeville, not far from Lieber.

Ron was assigned to the Birch 1 dorm, where he met Stephen Stanko. Stanko knew who Ron was and what he had done. They soon became friends. Stanko told Ron he should not have dropped the lawsuit. "I want you to let me do it," Stanko insisted. Ron disagreed, saying he was close to being released and did not want to jeopardize his chances.

Ron played on Stanko's softball team at MacDougall, where each dorm fielded a squad. Ron said Stanko was a good ball player, and very intelligent, but something was different about him. Ron and the others respected Stanko but knew it was best not to cross him. He said another inmate once said something derogatory to Stanko, who did not hesitate to punch him in the face.

Ron remembers Stanko telling him, "A lot of people in here, Ron, they all claim this God stuff and they all go to church, claim jailhouse religion. They come to jail, grab a hold of the Bible, then get out and do the same stuff they did before they got here. I can tell you're different, Ron. Keep up the good work."

Stanko often encouraged him, Ron said, adding he didn't know what Stanko was in prison for and didn't ask. "That can get you hurt," he said. It's more acceptable to ask how much time they have left, but even that isn't the smartest thing to do, Ron said.

It was Ron's policy to never tell the truth if people asked him how much time he had left. "The people who are never getting out will mess with you, try to get you more time," he told me. "They don't want you to leave. They don't root for each other's freedom."

Ron was required by law to serve at least four-and-a-half years of his nine-year sentence. On good behavior, he could be released at that time. He had been denied parole twice because he was serving concurrent sentences, plus his crimes were against the police so he was deemed an exceptional danger to society.

Counting down the days was common among inmates, and Ron was no different. But he worried the state might bring back the charges against him prior to the mistrial. He feared prosecutors would wait until he was close to leaving prison then slap him with a charge of assault with intent to kill. If so, he'd be stuck in prison until the new trial.

Later, when Ron's possible release date was only days away, the word had gotten out that he was about to get out, and he was worried.

But trouble never came. Ron clearly remembers the release process. Typically, the clothes he wore when arrested would be returned to him. But they were bloody, full of holes, and torn because they were cut off of him at the crime scene. So, his wife, Kim, brought him a fresh change of clothes the day he was freed. Kim and Ron's mother greeted him outside the gates, and immediately went to a Mexican restaurant for a celebratory lunch. His Sunday school teacher, who had visited him often in prison, met them there.

Ron's plan was to connect with his church, then find a job. He was fortunate. The church hired him to pull up carpet. That was in April 2004. He was 36 years old, was paid 10 dollars an hour, and was thankful. He was on probation for the next two-and-a-half years.

It wasn't hard for Ron to stay out of trouble. He was a changed man, and not once did he want to take any illegal drugs. He went out of his way to avoid his old hangouts. But after his church job was completed, he had a difficult time finding a new one. Hiring a felon is not on many employers' to-do list. On every job application, there is a question that asks, "Have you ever been convicted of a crime?"

So, Ron started his own landscaping and asphalt company. He got the money needed for the equipment from his mother-in-law. She believed in him. "I was lucky because I had people in my corner. A lot of guys don't have people willing to help them when they get out, and that's why they end up back in prison. Nobody disciplined me the way they should have when I was a kid. Prison helped me."

When he was a child, Ron remembers waiting in the car with one of his brothers while their mother went inside a store for groceries. Ron somehow managed to shift the car into neutral and it slowly rolled backwards. His brother jumped out, ran behind the vehicle, and tried to stop it. He slipped and fell on his stomach and the car rolled over him. His brother had back trouble for the rest of his life. Ron said chronic pain and a constant need for medication led to his brother's suicide.

Two years after Ron was released from prison, tragedy struck again when another one of his brothers killed himself. Two brothers. Two suicides. Tough. Six months later, Ron went to the hospital to visit an ailing member of his church. While there he reconnected with a man who he had first met while in prison. The man had worked in the prison, recognized Ron, and struck up a conversation.

"You should become a part of our team," he said. Ron agreed and soon found himself filling out Lieber's volunteer-services application, which included the following questions:

— Have you ever been arrested?

— Have you ever been charged with a crime?

— Have you ever been convicted of a crime?

If the applicant answered yes to any of those questions, there was space for his reply. Ron said he was truthful in answering them, but the spaces were too small to include all of his arrests, charges, and convictions. So Ron listed only three. Consequently, his application was denied.

Ron enlisted the help of a friend in the police department who wrote a letter to prison authorities explaining what had happened. Attached was a copy of Ron's extensive rap sheet. Realizing that he wasn't attempting to deceive them, the authorities agreed to allow Ron to return as part of the ministry team.

Ron visited Lieber as well as other prisons and enjoyed his work primarily because he could relate to inmates and felt he was an asset to the ministry. He had known some of the inmates previously. He had credibility with them; he gave them hope. One of those men was Stephen Stanko.

Ron was watching the local news one evening when he saw that Stanko had been sentenced to death for the murder of a girlfriend, the assault of her daughter and the murder an elderly man. He knew that Stanko would be lodged on death row at Lieber. So he decided to try to get in for a visit.

"Good to see you, Ron. I've thought about you often. I knew you'd be the guy who made it!" Stanko said when Ron arrived at his cell on death row.

Years later, Ron suggested that I go on death row and meet Stanko. "Oh great," I had responded. "You thought I would get along well with a man who committed such egregious crimes? That's comforting."

"No, man. He's the only one in there on your intellectual level," Ron said. "You're both smart guys. He has degrees and has written books. I thought you would connect."

Ron worked on the prison ministry team from 2006 until 2016 and often shared his story at local churches. But not now.

"I don't enjoy it anymore," he said. Most people who heard him were too judgmental. "They could not relate. All they wanted was to hear a good story. They don't gain anything from it."

"Why did you try then?" I asked.

"It was the only opportunity I had. I thought I was making a difference," he said, adding that his focus now is on helping young students stay out of trouble. "They're young and need to hear it."

Ron applied for a pardon in 2017 although he did not think it would be granted. He told his story to the South Carolina Parole and Pardon Board and was shocked by the response. He was granted a full pardon, thrilled and filled with emotion, so much so he was asked to calm down in the hallway after leaving the room. The ruling did not erase his record but provided him a pardon certificate to show potential employers. It says the state has forgiven him for his crimes.

"God has forgiven me and so has the state," he said. But he still sees people he has known for years who try to avoid him. "They see me as the person I was 20 years ago. It's sad, but I get it. They don't need me, and I don't need them. Life goes on."

One afternoon at the gym shortly after his release, Ron approached a man he had recognized from his past and tapped him on the shoulder. When the man turned around, Ron said, "Hey, is your name Glenn?"

"Yes, it is," the man said.

"I'm Ron Burris. You shot me seven years ago."

Glenn's face turned pale and instinctively he reached for his waistband before realizing he had no weapon.

"Don't worry, man," Ron said. "I'm not here to cause any problems. I wanted to tell you that I'm sorry for what I put you through that day, and I don't blame you for shooting me."

"I was just doing what I had to do," the off-duty police officer said.

"I would have done the same thing. No hard feelings on my end," Ron said.

Seven years ago they had nearly killed each other. That day they shook hands.

Ron's wife, Kim, supported him through it all, and he vows she's the only reason he's alive and well today. "Most women, probably 95 percent of them, would not have stuck by their man's side if they went through what I put her through," he said.

The Burrises have two daughters, ages 13 and 10, who give his life purpose, and they know about their father's past. "They know Daddy grew up in cars and slept in cars. They know about my drug use. They know some of the more private things I've had to deal with … I'm from the school of hard knocks and I want my daughters to know right from wrong … I have a good heart and my kids do too. If my mom and dad had stayed together, things would have been different for me. I was taught to do things that were wrong by authority figures in my younger years … I'm trying to teach them all the things I wish I'd been taught."

Ron also supports capital punishment, saying: "I believe in the death penalty, but I also believe in forgiveness. I believe that anyone who violates a child has crushed that child's life. I know because it happened to me. I still can't pee in public urinals unless there's a divider between them. Sexual exploitation of a minor is worse than murder."

"Do all sexual predators deserve the death penalty?" I asked.

"Well, no, but if they take a life, then yes," he replied.

"Do you think people can turn their lives around like you did, or are some people hopeless?"

"There is therapy and help out there for everyone," he said, but taking someone's life is a different matter, he added.

"Do you think Stanko deserves the death penalty?"

Ron thought for a few moments and said, "Stanko does deserve the death penalty and I think he thinks that he deserves it, too. He knows what he did was totally wrong. But he does have that frontal lobe issue as well."

Ron thought for a few moments, then said: "You still have to be accountable for your actions, though. So yeah … I think he deserves it. He raped a girl, killed the girl's mom then killed an old man and stole his vehicle. You can't go around doing stuff like that … If they do away with the death penalty, what's to deter people from killing? You're going to see more of it if they do."

Ron also said that the penalty should be death by hanging. "Hang them in the street for everyone to see. That would be a deterrent." Realizing that he may have gone too far there, he thought for a few more moments, then said, "I don't know man. I don't know," and sighed.

Chapter 5

I was consumed with thoughts about prison in January 2017, especially the men on death row. The monotony of their lives in particular bothered me. I imagined myself as being a juror during their trials. Having to decide if a killer should be executed or spared is a serious dilemma for me. Today, a death sentence for most killers means life in prison in what amounts to solitary confinement, which is a bad idea.

No one deserves to have a severe mental illness. Most agree that those who are sick should be treated for it. Yet when a mass shooting occurs in the United States, a great debate ensues about the causes. If it is determined that the killer has mental problems, why lock him or her in a cage for life? Shouldn't they be treated instead? What if they are cured? Should they be returned to death row? Should they be allowed to go free some day?

Prison authorities have seen inmates leave death row on both feet far more frequently than being laid out in a body bag. In the United States, more than 150 people have been exonerated and freed from death row since 1976. That doesn't include those whose sentences were reduced, and they were placed in the general prison population. Between 1976 and 2013, a total of 8,466 death sentences were handed down in the United States, and 3,194 were overturned on appeal. 1,359 were executed – that's just 16 percent. Execution is in fact the third most likely outcome following a death sentence. Much more likely is the inmate to have their sentence reversed, or to remain on death row for decades. Those sentenced to death are almost three times as likely to see their death sentence overturned on appeal and to be resentenced to a lesser penalty than they are to be executed.

Life-and-death decisions are being made without life-and-death accuracy. And why is it that only murder is deemed the highest level of crime that deserves the most severe form of punishment? What about child molesters? Why isn't that crime a capital offense? If you were on a one-man jury of two separate cases with one, and only one, death sentence to hand out, who would get it — the child molester or the murderer?

— Case #1: A man walks into a store to rob the place and the clerk pulls a gun. The robber, who also has a gun, shoots the clerk once in the leg. The clerk later dies.

— Case #2: A drug addicted ex-felon who served 12 years in prison for rape is out on parole. He breaks into a home, ties up a man and his wife, then rapes their two five-year-old twin daughters in front of their parents.

Which criminal deserves the death penalty?

By law, it would be the robber in Case #1. But, like a doctor, a juror can't look at a patient and see cancer. A doctor is expected to look beyond the surface to make a proper diagnosis.

Ron and I arrived at Lieber at 3:45 p.m. on Monday, January 30, 2017. It was my third visit. A white school bus with a blue stripe the length of each side was there when we arrived. There was nothing on the bus to identify it other than bars on the windows. Ron said it was a prison transport vehicle, and that inmates were inside. He knew what he was talking about. He had been a passenger on a prison bus full of inmates. He knew the emptiness most of the men on that bus were feeling at the time.

I was calm and confident as I cleared security. Ron insisted that I go first, "in case anything happens." I assumed he meant that he had my back. He always seemed to have my back when we were "behind bars." A woman gave me a bin like those used when going through airport security. I quickly removed my belt, shoes, and coat, emptied my pockets, and put everything in the bin for scanning.

"Where are you going today?" she asked.

"Death row," I said.

"I've never seen you here before," she said.

"This is my third time," I said, trying to sound convincing.

She seemed skeptical and asked for my name. After I told her who I was she went into another room and soon returned. "You're not on the list."

"I was here three weeks ago, and I was on the list then. I didn't have any problems getting in," I said.

"Well, you're not on it anymore," she said. "I don't know what to tell you."

She could see that I was frustrated. "What organization are you with?"

"I'm not with an organization. The chaplain cleared me."

"Which chaplain?"

I told her the chaplain's name.

"He's not here," she said, and stared at me.

I sighed, obviously frustrated. She went back into the other room for another minute and returned with some paperwork. "Here you are. I found you."

"What should I say next time to avoid this confusion?" I asked.

"Tell whoever is here that you are on the revised list."

The revised list? I wondered why "the revised list" wasn't "the list" but didn't ask.

She ran my bin through the scanner and pointed to the metal detector. After I cleared it, she patted me down and returned my belongings. At the next gate I inserted my driver's license into a slot and my visitor's badge came out. But I didn't consider myself a visitor anymore. I was not a friend of anyone on death row. I was not a relative of any of them either. I was not there for crumpets and tea. I was there on a mission that was not about spreading the Gospel. Yet I was a visitor just the same.

The chaplain wasn't there at the time, so Ron and I didn't go to the chapel. We took the walkway to the main lobby. The white sign noted that a total of 1,210 people were living at Lieber this time — nine less than on my previous visit. Steps in the right direction, I suppose. Baby steps, but steps, nonetheless.

As we entered the maximum-security building, I saw 10 or so inmates standing against the long white wall. Their hands and legs were shackled. A corrections officer was watching over them. I felt unsettled while walking past them, as if I was looking at a lineup and someone was expecting me to identify the perpetrator. I suppose anyone I pointed at would have been a correct answer. I made no eye contact as we walked past toward the red "Death Row" sign. The guard at the door was young — in his mid-20s maybe — and wore a protective vest. He asked if we were there to visit. I wanted to say "no," but said "yes."

"OK. Be careful," the guard said. "I ask that you stand back as far as you can from the cells — away from arms' reach. A guard was stabbed. OK?"

"Yes, sir," I said. I had heard this before. The stab-proof vests hanging on the wall made more sense this time, but I opted not to wear one. I did not want the inmates to think I was afraid.

I entered the lobby, got another pat-down, then checked the board that notes each inmate and his cell. I chose the right side of the block where Stanko, Moore, Big Johnny, and Chemo Guy lived. They had been talkative and seemed to trust me. The door to the right side opened and I walked into the square room with two floors. From that vantage point, I could see all the cells, including the fenced-off one at the bottom right.

"Don't look at him," Ron said about the man who was inside it.

The two staircases are on each side of the room, and everything is made of steel and concrete — the floor, the stairs, the cells, the doors — everything. I went up the stairs on the left. The inmate I saw first was Richard Moore, the man from Michigan, sitting at his desk eating, just like he was doing last time I was there.

"Michigander," I said. "Hey man, do you eat all day or what?"

He laughed and stood up. "What's going on, Steve? Nah, I do other stuff, but yeah, I do eat a lot. Today is steak-flavored-meat day. I just got done working out."

"Were you outside?"

Richard laughed. "No. Right here man." He pointed to the floor of his cell where he had four towels laid out. "My workouts get done in here — 100 burpees, 100 push-ups, and 100 sit-ups in 20 minutes. I'm working my way down to 15 minutes." He looked at me and added, "You've gotten some sun."

"I've been playing a little golf."

Richard asked if I had been working out.

"Not any more than usual."

We talked about the conditions in there (they all say how bad it is) and after about five minutes I moved on. A few cells down was Stephen Stanko, who was sitting at his desk. He wore earbuds and was writing. I saw a lot of paperwork that appeared to be legal documents and correspondence, which he takes out every morning and puts back in the same order in the evening.

"Mr. Stanko…" I said. He jerked his head around thinking I was a prison guard. When he realized it was me, he removed his earbuds, got up and walked over, and we shook hands.

"Steve. How's it going, man?"

"I'm good, how are you doing?" I said, which I later thought was a rather odd question for someone living on death row.

Stanko said he was writing an article for a doctor whose name I don't recall. We talked for a while and I mentioned that I saw the *48 Hours* television special about him. He crossed his arms and nodded his head.

"And …?" he asked.

I said it was interesting and asked what he thought of it.

He said the show did a better job of telling his story than *Dateline*, another television show on which he was interviewed. He said the producers of *48 Hours* interviewed him for three days in a room that looked like the inside of a spaceship. They filmed him from numerous angles and asked the same basic questions about his life and crimes until they got what they wanted, adding he thought it was a pretty good job. The name of the episode is "Murder on His Mind."

We talked about his health — more specifically about brain injuries and how they affect people, including players in the National Football League. I'm not going to go into details here because Stanko's case — like those of others facing the death penalty — is under appeal.

Stanko also said *48 Hours* reported that, following the murders, he drove to Augusta, Georgia, during the Masters golf tournament, which is held there annually. He said he went to a bar, met a woman and struck up a friendship. He said he wanted to prove to himself that he was not a monster. "I went to church with her for God's sake," he said.

Her friend eventually saw him on a television news report and notified the police. "They picked me up in a shopping mall," Stanko said. "I was in there getting something to eat, and when I came out, they arrested me. Years later, I was sitting in this cell and got a letter from that girl. She thanked me for not killing her." He said he wrote her back saying she was never in danger.

Stanko also told me his version of what happened. The details were vivid, and I cringed a little as I stood there listening to him. I asked if he believed in the death penalty. He said that he did. "There are plenty of people in here that have told me that they'd kill again if they got out. They deserve the death penalty."

"During your appeals process, do you think you'll give up and say, 'Screw this, just kill me?'" I asked.

"I don't think so. I'll continue to write and keep to my schedule. If it ever comes to it, though, I'll choose the electric chair."

"Why not lethal injection?" I asked.

His answer was rather odd: "The prison hates the electric chair. The officers can't stand it. It's the most traumatizing to watch. The body reacts and contorts violently. It's painful to see."

He also talked about how expensive it was to keep people like him on the row. It was clear that he had given his situation a lot of thought. He had an immediate answer for every question I had, which is understandable. He has a lot of time to think about such things while living in a 12-foot-by-7-foot cell day after day and seldom leaving it.

As our conversation was about to end, I was startled by a fast-moving object coming down the hall. As I said, death row is usually a rather quiet place where everything seems to be slow and calculated. Had someone gotten out of a cell? Was he coming after me?

That was the moment I learned that death row residents have microwave service. It arrives on top of a rolling cart. "Coming down," an inmate yelled as he pushed the cart down the row. If an inmate wants to heat up his food, he reaches out and grabs the cart. But on that day, the cart had gotten out of hand and was headed for the stairs. A guard was chasing after it and stopped the contraption before it went off the cliff, so to speak.

After everything quieted down again, I asked one more question of Mr. Stanko. "What's the main problem with South Carolina's prison system?"

"A big one is the classification system ... Well, not the system itself, but the fact that they ignore it," he said. "They put new prison inmates in the wrong pods and with the wrong people ... First, they ask if you're in a gang, then ask if you have any family members in the prison, and if you have enemies here — things like that — but they disregard what you say because there aren't enough beds. New inmates go wherever there's an open bed."

"It's also about intimidation," he added. But I didn't press Stanko for further explanation. I told him it was good talking to him and appreciated his being so open with me. I was tired, but I also wanted to go downstairs and talk to Big Johnny.

When I got there, Big Johnny was leaning against his door. His huge arms and hands hung out through the food tray slot. All of the inmates, the ones who want to talk anyway, seemed to be leaning against the inside of their doors when I was there. Picture yourself in a pet store. As you walk by, most of the dogs come to the front of their cages and try to get your attention. It's like that on death row.

Johnny is a very big man. Shaking his hand was like grappling with a grizzly bear, I suppose. He always wore a white tank top, white shorts, and a black beanie. Yet he is soft spoken and unintimidating, and smiles a lot.

"Johnny. How are you man?"

"Another day in paradise," he said.

"Do you believe in the death penalty?" As far as ice breakers go, that one wasn't my best.

"No."

"Did you believe in it before you were sentenced to death?"

"No. Never have. Since I've been in here (1995), I've seen 30 guys leave and not come back."

"Wow. What's that like?"

"It's tough. The mood is somber in here the week before and the week after an execution."

Death row inmates were moved in 1997 to Lieber from the state prison in Columbia. Big Johnny was among them.

"What was it like the day they moved you guys from Columbia to this prison?" I asked.

"It was unexpected. They woke us up real early by throwing two duffel bags into each cell and telling us to pack up. We stuffed all of our possessions into those bags, they shackled us, then loaded us on buses. They had a convoy of cars in front and behind our buses. They shut down I-26 while they drove us down here, and I could hear helicopters above. It's worse here than it was there. I was too large for the handcuffs and shackles, so it was very uncomfortable. When they move us anywhere, they put a chain around our waists and handcuff us so that our wrists are tight against our stomachs. They shackle our feet, too. My wrists are big, and it was painful. They don't care, though."

"Does the A/C work in here?" I asked.

"Sometimes. It gets crazy hot here in the summer. I sweat real bad too, so it's not fun."

After talking with Big Johnny, I said hello to Chemo Guy, his next-door neighbor. I asked him if he was feeling any better.

"Nope," Chemo Guy said. "I'm going to go lay down now. I'll catch up with you next time."

I was tired too. As I was leaving the block that day, I saw an old man in a wheelchair being pushed by an inmate. I wondered if he was somebody's grandfather who had stopped in for a visit. Then I noticed that the man in the chair was wearing a tan prison shirt and pants. He looked to be at least 80 years old.

That's when I concluded that South Carolina's system of justice doesn't care how old a man is. A life sentence is a life sentence. I recalled an incident at my school during an awards ceremony a couple of weeks prior to that day at Lieber. I was standing on the stage passing out certificates to deserving students. Afterward, a parent told me that a woman sitting behind him told her husband, "That's the guy who went to prison," and she pointed at me.

I laughed and said, "You made sure she knew that I wasn't an inmate, right?"

But I wasn't laughing as I was leaving after my third visit to Lieber. It was 6:45 p.m. when I traded in my badge for my driver's license. Every time the guard returned my personal belongings and I walked out of those prison gates, I thought about the 1,200 or so people I had left behind. They would have given almost anything to trade places with me. When I got home, I made a list of more questions to ask.

Chapter 6

Ridgeville, South Carolina, is not on your way to anywhere. After exiting I-26, you take narrow roads this way and that, pass a few houses and small churches, and turn left on a county road through a gate into Lieber. I always drove my pickup truck to the prison and Ron always rode shotgun. "Riding shotgun" is not quite right considering the circumstances, but you get what I mean.

Upon arrival Ron would share a prayer, which went something like: "Lord, please look over us as we enter this maximum-security prison full of killers. My friend Steve hasn't said anything for a while so I know he's nervous. Bless him with courage and bravery, but mostly don't let us die in this prison today."

We would say "Amen" and smile. It was Ron's way of asking God to help us lighten up before submerging ourselves in a place that sucks the life out of most visitors — and I appreciated his thoughtfulness.

I had no problems getting in on my fourth visit. I had become a regular, a man who runs his shoes through the x-ray machine one sole at a time. The guards realized it was unnecessary to pat me down so close to my meat and potatoes, and how I like my eggs — not touching anything else on my plate, so to speak. I felt like Norm on the television sitcom *Cheers*. Everyone knew my name. (Not really, but I was certainly a lot more comfortable going directly to death row, which sounds odd.)

This time, the overall inmate count had increased by 15, to 1,225. After leaving the main lobby, clearing both sets of electric doors, and reaching the walkway to the prison's maximum-security section, I noticed two African-American inmates sitting on white lawn chairs and talking to each other. They looked up at us as we approached and asked if we were headed to the row.

One appeared to be in his 60s and the other in his 40s. The older man said he had been on death row for 15 years before being moved to the general population seven years ago. He said he knew of South Carolina's infamous murderer Pee Wee Gaskins, who also lived on the row before being executed in the electric chair in 1991.

Gaskins was tried on eight murder charges in 1976 and found guilty after the jury deliberated for four days. He was sentenced to death, but it was later commuted to life to conform to US Supreme Court guidelines. But in 1982 Gaskins planted a small bomb into a radio that belonged to fellow inmate Rudolph Tyner, who had murdered an elderly couple during a bungled store robbery. Gaskins had figured out how to detonate the bomb from his own cell and literally blew the man's head off. It was an in-house hit job.

Gaskins first tried to kill Tyner by having the man's meals laced with poison. That didn't work, so he rigged the portable radio and gave it to Tyner, saying it would allow the two of them to communicate with each other between their cells. Tyner followed Gaskins' instructions to hold a speaker (secretly laden with C-4 plastic explosive) to his ear. At an agreed upon time, Gaskins detonated the bomb.

"The last thing he heard was me laughing," Gaskins was quoted as saying following the second trial, in which he was found guilty and sentenced to death. Gaskins told his life story to Wilton Earle, who wrote a biography about him titled *Final Truth*. Gaskins claimed he committed as many as 110 murders, including that of a 13-year-old daughter of a state senator from Sumter, South Carolina. He also said he possessed "a special mind" that gave him permission to kill people. Needless to say, many of Gaskins' claims remain unverified.

Anyway, the inmate that said he knew Gaskins added that some of Tyner's brains were still on the wall of a cell somewhere inside the place where it happened, which is also unverified.

This time on death row I went to see William Bell, who had been there for 28 years — most of that time in solitary confinement. He was 19 years old when he was arrested for his role in the murder of an elementary school principal. Bell acted as if he knew I was coming to see him. He stood smiling against the bars. His hair was cut in a short, well-groomed afro, and he wore a white T-shirt and white long underwear. I shook his hand.

"Did you come here with Ron?" he asked.

"Yes."

"He told me that I should talk to you sometime. Glad you're here."

I was carrying a yellow pad and a pen, and asked if it was OK to take notes.

"I don't care what you do," Bell said.

"It's been 28 years in this place. How do you do it?" I asked him.

"I have a routine and I try to stick to it. Every day is the same for me pretty much."

"Do you mind walking me through a typical day?" I asked.

He said it starts at 2 a.m. with exercise: 200 burpees, 300 push-ups, 200 curls. He showed me what he uses for curls: a bucket of water with a torn-off bed sheet wrapped around it for handles.

Next he rests and reads from 4 to 6 a.m., when the guards and other workers change shifts. He said it's noisy in the mornings because most of the inmates are waking up and talking as they wait for breakfast, which is served until 8 a.m.

Next he takes a shower, if permitted. A two-hour recreation period follows when inmates are allowed to go outside — usually three times a week into the small, containment areas known as "dog runs." He said the inmates usually play checkers, chess, or whatever through the wires with whoever is in an adjacent cage. Since the guards move inmates one at a time, it takes a couple of hours to cycle all the inmates through the stations.

From 9 to 11 a.m. Bell watches television or listens to the radio. "I always watch *The Young and the Restless*. I love that show; been my favorite forever," he said. He also enjoys Westerns including *Bonanza* and *Gunsmoke*. He said *Star Trek* comes on at 8 p.m.

Lunch is served from 11 a.m. to 12 p.m. Inmates spend afternoons sleeping, reading mail, listening to the radio, and not much else. Supper is served around 5 p.m. and bedtime begins at 8 p.m. unless *Star Trek* is on. That basically has been William Bell's daily routine for the last 28 years.

Bell asked what people say when they find out I have visited death row. I said they ask if the inmates are remorseful for their crimes. "I usually say you do seem to have feelings of remorse."

Bell agreed. "My role in the death of an elementary principal is why I'm here. He was shot and killed late at night while he was walking to his car from the school."

I wasn't sure if he was messing with me or not. I let him finish his story before telling him my line of work.

Bell: "The night started with me and a couple of my boys hanging out at the house. We were partying, and decided to walk to the club. Between the house and the club is the elementary school. We were walking down the street and noticed a car parked outside the building. My boy started messing with the lock. I told him to leave it alone, to keep walking so we continued on to the club.

"About halfway between the school and the club, we heard a gunshot coming from the club. We stopped and asked each other, "Do we really want to get into this tonight?" We turned around and started walking back to the house. When we got to the school, my boy wanted to see who was inside so late at night. He walked around the entire school while my other buddy and me waited out front. When he got back, we noticed a guy coming out of the door. One of my boys said, "He probably has a wallet on him. Let's get it."

"We robbed the guy and he was shot. We took off back to the house. I watched the news later and all they were talking about was the principal who was shot outside the school. They didn't say anything about him being dead. I was praying to God the man would live. I was awakened by my sister who said to come see what was on the news. 'Damn man! They shootin' principals now? What the hell is going on out there?' she said.

"She had no idea I was involved. Later, the police came and took us all in. I can't tell you how many times I've gone over that night in my head," Bell said.

"How did they know it was you guys who did it?" I asked.

"A girl from the apartments by the school told them she saw us in the area that night and saw us running from the scene."

"How did they prove it was you?"

"They found my fingerprints on his car."

"Did your friends also get the death penalty?"

"Me and the shooter got it. He was executed in 2002 and the other guy was paroled."

I told Bell that I was an assistant principal of an elementary school. "I walk to my car in the dark at night often. What you just described hits close to home."

"Wow. Really? Good for you, man. That's great," Bell said.

That was not the response that I had expected. He didn't seem to appreciate the irony of my being there. I get goosebumps when I talk about it. Was he being truthful? I looked it up later on casetext. com and this is what I read:

The victim in this case, Dennis Hepler, was the principal of West Franklin Street Elementary School in Anderson, South Carolina. His body was found outside the school around 1 a.m. on Sep. 1, 1988. He had been shot twice with a .25 caliber pistol, once in the back and once in the back of the head. The appellant's fingerprints were found on the victim's red car, which was parked on the street in front of the school. Two witnesses from a nearby apartment complex placed appellant in the area between 10 and 11 p.m. on Aug. 31 with John Glen and Kevin Young.

"Why are you still alive?" I asked. "Why haven't they killed you yet?"

"Appeals, appeals, appeals. Lengthy appeals," Bell said. "My lawyer told me in January 2003 that in November of that year they would schedule an execution date. That came and went. Caseloads are so heavy that we get pushed to the bottom of the pile most of the time. But a few months ago, my case was overturned, and I'm going to serve life in prison instead. I should be out of here (death row) by the end of the summer and in general population. We proved my mental-health case. You can't sentence someone who is mentally retarded (the court still uses that term) to death, so I got life in prison. Once the paperwork goes through and is signed, I'll be in general population. I've never seen general population in prison … Can you believe that?"

He wasn't lying. William Bell is a first-time offender who went straight to death row. He was transferred in 1997 when the row was moved to Lieber from Broad River Correctional Institution in Columbia. Bell had not had physical contact with friends or family members in 20 years. Now he is allowed one visitor per week who can talk with him through a plexiglass window. He said a visitor's request is approved or denied based on available time slots. He said his sisters come to see him every now and again.

"I talk to my nieces pretty regularly on the phone, though. They were babies when I was arrested, so they only know me from in here." He said that when he was young his role models were ex-cons. "If you got out of prison, you were perceived as tough. Isn't that insane? I looked up to them because they spent time in prison and survived … But I didn't want my nieces thinking that way. I told them to look at the world differently than I did. They're grown now and live productive lives. I'm proud of them … I tell them that all the time."

"How many people have you known in here who have been executed?"

"Somewhere around 50," Bell said, adding he had been on death row for about a week when the first man was taken away. "I had no idea what was going on … I watched him go from cell to cell talking to every inmate. My neighbors said he would be taken to the death chamber and he was saying his goodbyes. I had no idea what to say to him. I had been in here for only a week … That's when it hit me how real this was. He got to my cell, I shook his hand, he looked at me, smiled and said: 'I know where I'm going and I'm OK with it.'

"That's the reality of this place. We're real people, and that's the side of this place that nobody knows about or sees. Death row is the best kept secret in the world."

"What's the worst part of being in here?" I asked.

He thought for a few moments and said, "The dreams, man, I have dreams about freedom all the time … There's one in particular that I have more than any other: I'm being escorted to the death chamber, but the death chamber is located in the back of my elementary school. I'm walking down the hallway to the back of the school when I escape the shackles. I run as fast as I can and jump over the fence behind the school and I am free. Waking up from that dream is the worst feeling."

"Why do you think it's in your elementary school?"

"Those were the best times of my life. That's when I was the happiest. I wasn't in trouble. I had a lot of friends and good teachers. … But that dream is the same every single time. Then I wake up and I'm still here. It's a terrible feeling."

"What are the good times in here? When are you happiest?" I asked.

"When I talk to people, like we're doing right now."

"Are there a lot of people that come in and talk to you guys like I'm doing right now?"

"Not a lot … Maybe once or twice a week. A lot of times they'll come in and just say "Hi" and move on," he said.

"The guards tell me to make sure I stand back, away from the bars when I'm in here, so I don't open myself up to getting hurt by one of you. What do you think about that?" I asked.

"You don't have anything to worry about, with me at least. There are some people in here that have shanked the guards and tried to kill them, but the day one of the volunteers gets hurt in here will be a very bad day … They wouldn't allow y'all back in here if one of you got injured and we know that. You don't have anything to worry about. You are being sized up in here, though, believe that. We can sense fake. You're being assessed by everyone … When we see genuine, it reminds us that we're human."

During the hour or so I was talking with William Bell, the rolling microwave was in great demand. It was passed by me several times as the prisoners rolled it down the hallway. The inmates are adept at maneuvering both the telephone and microwave carts. I'd look down the row and see their arms and hands sticking out from the cells, then someone would holler "Heads up, coming down." Soon one of the carts went by. They are very good about knowing the perfect amount of force to roll it with depending on which cell has requested it. The South Carolina Death Row Shuffleboard Team would be a force to be reckoned with. Numbers-wise, Texas, Florida and California would be tough to match up against, but I wouldn't overlook South Carolina.

Bell asked me what people on the outside thought about people on the row, saying, "I don't know much about what the public thinks of us. I did see a show one time about a girl who was upset because she couldn't afford to get a college education while the government allowed prisoners college courses for free. That kind of got under my skin … The majority of prisoners will be released one day … She should want us to get an education."

Me: "Did you get an education in here?"

Bell: "They won't let death row inmates go to class or to work. They tell us we don't need it. A lot of us read and educate ourselves, but we can't get an official certificate in here."

Me: "One debate that comes up about capital punishment is whether or not the death penalty deters crime. What are your thoughts on that?"

Bell: "Nobody goes into a situation thinking they'll get caught. You don't drive faster than the speed limit thinking you'll get caught. It's not a risk/reward thing. People commit crimes for a reason. People kill people for a reason. They're not good reasons, but to them, there is a reason. Everybody in here who is guilty can tell you why they did it. You won't like or agree with it, but they will give you a reason. See what I'm saying? That man was killed because we wanted his money. It's not right, but we weren't thinking about the death penalty at that moment, I can promise you that. We didn't think we would get caught. We were stupid. Have you seen the show *Scared Straight* where they bring the kids in the prison and try to scare them off their current life path?"

I told him that I had seen it.

"Those kids think general population is the last stop in prison. They should bring those kids in here and see what the real last stop is like. I convinced the warden to bring a group of kids back here a while ago, but he would only allow them in the lobby. He wouldn't bring them all the way in to see the cells or any of the other inmates back here where we are now. They took me in shackles into the lobby to talk to them.

"There were 10 of them and they were young. I told them what it was like in here, but they didn't get it. They just stared at me. I gave them details about the lethal injection. I told them that Hollywood makes it out to be a peaceful way to die. It's not. There are actually three injections. The first one is a sedative. The second one is a paralyzer. The third one stops your heart. You are in pain the whole time, but your body doesn't physically react because its paralyzed. They didn't ask any questions. I could tell it wasn't sinking in.

"The only thing I heard was one kid say, "This ain't going to be me." That right there answers your question about whether or not the death penalty deters crime. Hell no it doesn't! Nobody ever thinks it will happen to them."

I asked Bell what advice he would give a young person on his first day in death row.

"I would tell him not to be afraid to talk to people and to ask questions. Before I came in here, I was taught to keep my mouth shut, stand up for myself if I had to, and not get too close to anyone. That's not true. Death row is different than general population. This is survival. If you keep to yourself, you'll go insane quickly. People come in here and they have nothing. It takes a few days to get your pin number for the phone, so you can't call anyone or have anybody send you stuff. You literally walk in here with nothing but the prison-issued clothes on your back. That's why I have these put together ready to go…"

He stepped over to his desk, reached in a drawer, pulled out three gallon-sized plastic bags with items inside and brought them to me.

"These are care packages that I have ready to go for new people that come in. Each one has toothpaste, deodorant, a pen, paper, a hat and a face cloth: Things you need but don't have when you get here. I've given out a lot of these in the past 28 years. Someone gave one to me when I got here, and I was grateful. It's a quick and easy way to show someone that they're not alone; that we're all in this together. People share stuff all the time: shampoo, food, books, anything you need that someone can lend you."

Random acts of kindness are valuable no matter where you are in this world. That's a good reminder that somewhere, someone is praying for the things you're taking for granted.

I thanked William Bell for being so open and answering all of my questions. He told me to come back soon and that I can ask him anything. I learned a lot from him that day. Think about it: He has spent 28 years in what is more or less solitary confinement — which is worse than death. It's cruel and unusual punishment. It affects a person's psyche, and could result in even more violence. But William Bell seemed to be OK psychologically. Why? I don't know.

I also stopped at Stanko's cell and talked to him briefly. He was writing as usual when I walked up. After a couple minutes of small talk, I asked if he would accept a life sentence if offered.

"Probably not if it meant I was going to stay at Lieber. I know how this yard works. It's terrible out there. These kids don't know the code. They just stab people. When I was in the general population, we would fight to settle our scores. Now, they stab and kill. It would end badly for me if I went back in there. These kids steal stuff from other inmates, and nothing happens to them. I wouldn't let them do that to me."

I told him I was glad he brought that up. "In the *48 Hours* story they did on you, you said you were in more than 30 fights in prison, but the guards went on the stand and said they didn't have any record of you getting into fights. Why is that?"

"They don't report them most of the time," he said. "We would fight out of sight of the guards. When they did see us, we'd stop fighting. Nobody snitched because they knew what would happen if they did. It's different now, though. Like I said, people stab each other and there is physical evidence that the guards can't ignore …"

"Are there any TV shows that you watch daily?" I asked.

"I never miss *Ellen*. You can't watch her show and be upset. She's always happy. A lot of people don't watch certain shows because they say it's fake. But that's the reason why I do watch TV: It's an escape from reality. Anytime I can escape this place in my mind, I take advantage of it. *Ellen* gives me the opportunity to smile and be happy and I don't want to miss that."

On my way out, I stopped to talk to Richard Moore, the inmate from Michigan who killed a store clerk during a robbery. I had a pen and pad in hand. He asked if I was writing a book, which surprised me. I said I was noting my observations because people on the outside ask me about the place and I want to be accurate. I asked if he minded my taking notes.

"Are you for or against it?" Moore responded.

"For or against what?"

"This. In here. Everything. The death penalty," he said.

"If you're asking about the death penalty, I'm against it."

"OK … I'll answer your questions," Moore said.

But he didn't have much more to say during the 10 minutes or so we talked until the evening meals were served in white, to-go boxes — chicken, cabbage, and rice. Some of the inmates ate, others did not. I was starving, but was not offered a meal, so I left.

Chapter 7

I didn't start my journey into the darkness of death row wanting to write a book or get my name in the newspaper. I wanted to help and was merely curious — mostly about the accuracy of television specials and movies about prison life — and I knew someone who offered to get me in. After four visits to Lieber I was somewhat familiar with the living conditions of prisoners in the general population. But now I know a lot about life on death row, which several of those in residence say is one of the best-kept secrets anywhere.

Cameras are not allowed in the hands of visitors to death row. Photos and film footage of the place are seldom seen. In addition, windows are small, narrow, and few and far between. I was as surprised as I am grateful that authorities allowed me to go in. I'm also glad that I can use words to shed light on the place.

After my first time in the institution, I knew I wanted to go back, but didn't have high expectations of getting permission. When I got word that I could return, I made a list of questions and soon added more from family and friends. With each visit my nerves calmed when I was with the inmates. I soon gained confidence to ask them just about anything. But I never initiated conversation about their specific crimes. Many of them told me why they were there, and allowed me to dig deeper into their lives. Their names, faces, and convictions are public knowledge, easily obtained through a Google search, so my writing about it here should not be considered distributing proprietary information.

I quickly learned to listen more, talk less, and treat each man with respect. A handshake and addressing each by name meant a lot to them. I didn't appear to be nervous or intimidated, although I was initially. I also learned there is nothing I could do to prepare myself for talking face-to-face with a convicted murderer for the first time.

Being in the business of teaching and administering public schools, I recall the tried-and-true educators' saying: "They don't care how much you know until they know how much you care." This rings true on death row as well. I also looked into their cells for anything I could bring up in conversation to break the ice: a sticker of a sports team or college, a book, food, pictures, what they watch on television, anything I could talk about. Most visitors are clergymen and the conversations typically involve spiritual matters. I wanted to know what they thought about other issues. I was careful not to judge them and was not disrespectful if we disagreed. I asked tough questions. I wanted them to think before they answered. I didn't judge them or disrespectfully disagree with anything they said. They've already been judged.

Some of their answers were extremely disturbing. They told me about shockingly inhumane, horrendous events in their lives. I never lectured them, and I did not issue an opinion unless they asked. I stayed calm, welcoming, and attentive. I also have a good sense of humor, which helped. I enjoyed making them smile — lifting their spirits in an extremely depressing place.

One inmate said complaining gets him nowhere, and he tries to maintain a positive attitude. I told him that I could relate to that. "Parents complain to me when I sentence their child to recess detention — and here you are in this place for the next 300 years and you're smiling."

Gallows humor goes a long way on death row. "Tell that kid I'll serve his detention if he'll serve my death sentence," the inmate joked.

My fifth trip to death row — or to "permanent timeout," in school principal lingo — seemed as if it would be one of my last. I had no problem getting inside. The guard didn't check to see if my name was on the list. The whiteboard in the lobby noted there were 1,206 inmates in the institution. After walking through the long, white hallway toward the row and past the kitchen where they prepare the inmates' meals, I was almost knocked over by the stench. The menu must have consisted of "manager's choice" as the meal of the day. It smelled like it was some sort of mystery meat that had been around for a while.

I chose to visit the left side of the row this time, where I had not spent as much time. The left side is reputed to be home to the worst offenders. I don't know if that's true, but there are fewer inmates on the left side than on the right. I started on the lower level.

During my initial lap around the perimeter, I noticed one man was talking on the mobile phone while the others appeared to be sleeping. So I went upstairs to see Ron, who was talking to a short, angry-looking man named Stephen. Ron was keeping his distance from the man, which was unusual. Stephen stood with his back against the corner of his cell closest to the door. His arms were crossed and he was not smiling. My first impression of him was not outstanding. I would compare it to the feeling you get when you meet someone for the first time and they say they're from Ohio (no offense to anyone in Ohio, it's just a joke Michiganders and South Carolinians share). Or when you get a text message from someone and the text is green instead of blue. Or when you ask someone what time it is and they answer in military time. Or when you ask someone for directions and they use words like west and east instead of right and left. You get the point. Nothing we can't overcome, just not ideal. I patted Ron on the back as I walked past him as if to say, "Good luck, buddy."

I worked my way down three cells to an inmate named Marion, who said hello, obviously wanting to talk. While walking around the tiers, some of the offenders would look up from their bed or desk and simply smile or nod. That was their way of saying they weren't interested in having a conversation. If they were awake, none of them completely ignored me.

I had met Marion before and we had talked briefly. But I wasn't sure if he remembered. He'd been on the row for 12 years, convicted of killing his estranged wife. His story is on the Spartanburg-based website goupstate.com, posted on May 22, 2004:

The shots that killed Ruby Nell Lindsey as she tried to hide in a car at the Inman Police Department two years ago are still reverberating. Celeste Nesbitt's two daughters, 4 and 9 years old, were inches away from Lindsey when her estranged husband, Marion Lindsey, shot her to death in the back seat of Nesbitt's car on the night of Sept. 18, 2002.

A jury took just 15 minutes to convict Marion Lindsey of murder late Friday afternoon, setting the stage for a separate trial to determine whether he lives or dies. After the verdict, Inman resident Nesbitt said her oldest daughter was seated next to Nell Lindsey when three bullets crashed into her head, and is still traumatized by her early introduction to violent death. The girl and her younger sister's screams can be heard on a dramatic 911 tape of Nell Lindsey's call for help in the moments before Marion Lindsey shot into Nesbitt's car four times with a .38 special.

In the audio tape, which solicitor Trey Gowdy played for jurors Friday morning, the girls' piercing cries began after the first two shots through Nesbitt's tinted back window. They continued after Lindsey walked around to the driver's side and fired two more shots into the rear window. "If (the older daughter, now 11) hadn't ducked down into the floorboard, she would be dead now, too," Nesbitt said. "She was traumatized by this. She hasn't done well in school since it happened. She's had to undergo counseling. She suffers from manic/depression, and she's on medication."

As the closest eyewitness to the murder, Nesbitt was the prosecution's star witness. She testified that she was driving Nell Lindsey home from her job at Spartanburg Regional Medical Center — Lindsey's car was disabled — when they spotted Marion Lindsey in his girlfriend's car behind them. Nell Lindsey, 27, lived with her mother and her two sons were conceived with Marion Lindsey. Nesbitt testified that she drove into the driveway of a relative's home, then re-entered the street to encounter Marion Lindsey in his vehicle. She said Lindsey, who could not see through her tinted back seat windows, asked if she had seen his estranged wife. Aware that Marion and Nell Lindsey's marriage had been tumultuous, Nesbitt replied that she had not spoken to Mrs. Lindsey in days.

At one point, Nesbitt said, her youngest daughter leaned over into the front seat, looked outside and said hello to Marion Lindsey. Prosecutors later argued that this proved Lindsey knew at least one child was in the car when he fired into it. Nesbitt said Lindsey became suspicious, asking her to lower a rear window so he could see who was inside. She replied that the windows were broken and would not lower. When Lindsey exited his car, Nesbitt said, she sped away to the Inman Police Department. With Marion Lindsey in pursuit, she disregarded traffic signals and crossed a set of railroad tracks at high speed. Nesbitt said she jumped out of her car at the police department, but Nell Lindsey would not leave. She described watching Marion Lindsey shoot into the car, after which she (Nesbitt) crawled into a parked police car for cover. Police officer Bennie Godfrey testified that he wounded Lindsey after Lindsey pointed the .38 at him.

Marion was mild-mannered while we talked that day. "I've been wanting to ask you a question," he said to me. "How do kids have GPAs in middle school? I thought they don't get a GPA until high school? My daughter told me that she has a 3.6, but she's only in middle school. What exactly does that mean?"

I told him first that his daughter is very smart if she has a 3.6 GPA. I explained what the score meant and how she earned it. He nodded his head and smiled. I envisioned him talking to his daughter on the phone, and her telling him proudly that she had a 3.6. Marion surely told her that he was happy although he didn't really know what the numbers meant. I told him about high school credits, and how kids can earn them in middle school now.

"It can really help your daughter in the long run if she gets high school credits early because then she could start earning college credit early, saving a lot of money on tuition," I said.

"Thanks, man, I've been thinking about that," he said. He also saw that my shirt had my school's logo on the front. "How are things at Orange Grove? Do the kids bully each other a lot?" he asked.

"No, I'm lucky to work at a really good school. We don't have a lot of bullying. The teachers can spend more time teaching because the kids behave themselves."

"That's great," Marion said. "When I was in school, if we saw someone getting picked on, we'd stick up for them. 'Stop messin' with him,' we would say. Now, it seems, people don't speak up anymore. They're too scared they'll get beat up or something."

I told him times have certainly changed, but bullying is not as prevalent as the news makes it seem, like most other issues in television news today.

"You're probably right, but TV is the only way we stay connected to the outside world in here," Marion said. "They also talk about legalizing marijuana. I think they should legalize it. You ain't never heard of someone smoking a bunch of weed and going on a crime spree. People don't hurt people when they're high on weed. A lot of people smoke weed. You probably have some teachers in your school who go home after a long day and roll a doobie."

I smiled and said, "Yeah, you're probably right."

We also talked about the death penalty. "Do you believe in it?" I asked.

"I'm 50/50 on that. Some people deserve it. Serial killers should get it. I hate the way it's set up, though. There are no rules. If a prosecutor wants to pursue it, he can. If he wants to take it off the table or make a deal, he can do that. I was willing to take life in prison, but they never offered that to me."

"Why?"

"Because of all the publicity my case got. If it stays out of the news, they usually offer life without parole to avoid going to trial. If it gets a lot of coverage, the public wants death. If you get a young prosecutor who is trying to advance his career and get a death penalty case under his belt, there's a good chance that will happen. It depends on the media and the individual prosecutor. That's my issue — it should be given out fairly. But there are no rules. Then, when you go to trial, the jury thinks that if they sentence you to death, you're going be executed within a year or so. Half of us wouldn't be here right now if the jury knew how long it takes and how much money it costs taxpayers like you. Some people have been here for 30 years. If juries have that information, they wouldn't sentence us to death. The death penalty was originally intended for terrorists. Did you know that?"

"No," I said, and I still don't.

We had talked for 20 minutes when Ron called out saying inmate Stephen Bryant, who had the tough-to-crack exterior, wanted to speak to me. I thanked Marion for being so forthcoming. He thanked me for stopping by. When I got to the man's cell I saw that Ron continued to keep his distance from Bryant. I had earlier seen Ron showing Bryant his bullet wounds, which I thought was a great way to get a death row inmate to open up. It helps to have something in common, I suppose.

The following story about Bryant is also from the Spartanburg-based website goupstate.com, posted on September 11, 2008:

The killer taunted investigators, scrawling in blood on one dead man's wall: "Victim 4 in 2 weeks. Catch me if u can." He lit candles around the body and laughed when the man's daughter called and asked to speak with her father. "You can't," he told her. "I killed him three hours ago."

Investigators said they may never know why Stephen Bryant, who was on probation after 18 months in prison for burglary, started killing in 2004. He pleaded guilty last month to three murders and a nonfatal shooting in Sumter County, a mostly rural area in central South Carolina. A judge sentenced him to death today for one of the killings, and life in prison for the other two. As relatives and friends of his victims wept, Bryant hung his head — a contrast to earlier court appearances when he stared at prosecutors and mouthed obscenities. "Maybe now we can begin to get on with our lives," said Teresa Becker, a friend of one victim's family. "Not a day goes by when we don't think about what happened. It's been a long four years."

Bryant's three victims were found over a week, within 5 miles of each other in Sumter County where dirt and gravel roads crisscross in the woods between Shaw Air Force Base and a state forest. One other victim survived. Clinton Brown, then 56, was shot in the back while fishing from a riverbank. He drove himself to the hospital.

Defense attorney Jack Howle asked the judge to spare Bryant's life, saying he never recovered from sexual abuse as a child. Bryant began using drugs again about a month before the killings, including smoking marijuana joints after lacing them with bug spray. Bryant also wrote a long letter apologizing to one victim's widow.

The most chilling murder was that of Willard Tietjen, 62, who was shot nine times. Bryant confessed he knocked on Tietjen's door and told him his truck had overheated. The two spoke about religion and the Masons for hours before Bryant started shooting. He spent a few more hours ransacking the home, dipping the corner of a pot holder made by Tietjen's daughter in Tietjen's blood to scrawl messages, and using a pen to write other notes taunting investigators.

Tietjen's widow, Mildred, testified that Bryant answered her husband's cell phone, identified himself as the prowler and said her husband was dead. Tietjen's daughter, Kimberly Dees, said that when she called a few minutes later, he told her he was having a wonderful day. When she asked to speak to her dad, Bryant told her she couldn't because he'd killed him, then laughed as he hung up the phone.

Also killed during Bryant's spree was his pal, 36-year-old Clifton Gainey, who was shot in the back on a dirt road as he relieved himself, then again in the head as he raised his hand to shield his face. Bryant drove off in his truck with the steaks the men had just bought, prosecutors said.

Bryant also left Christopher Burgess, 35, on an isolated dirt road. His body was found the day after deputies questioned Bryant because the license plate on a truck making the strange stops around the county was traced back to him. Bryant told authorities the men threatened him, but investigators said they *have no evidence of that. A psychiatrist testified during the sentencing hearing that Bryant suffers from paranoia.*

Debbie DuRant said she figures Bryant is just evil. She said she saw it in his eyes when he drove up the half-mile driveway from a gravel road to her house claiming he was a contractor and couldn't find the house he was supposed to be working on. DuRant said she couldn't help him and asked him to please drive away slowly because her dogs were in the yard. It was a way for her to get his license plate number.

Gainey's body was found about a mile away a few days later. DuRant, her husband and two daughters, then in middle school, all slept in an upstairs bedroom for the next few days with their dogs and loaded guns in easy reach. The family packed up and stayed about 10 miles away in Sumter until Bryant was arrested, DuRant said. Even today, DuRant's oldest daughter, now a sophomore in college, won't stay in their home by herself. "I'm not scared of very much at all," DuRant said. "But for that week, we lived in absolute fear."

I did not know anything about Mr. Bryant or his crimes when Ron said to him, "Tell Steve what you just told me." I looked at Bryant, expecting him to start talking. He didn't look back. He just leaned against the wall, looked angry, and said nothing.

After a few moments of silence, I saw his bald head slowly move to his right. Suddenly he stared into my eyes. If there hadn't been bars between us, I would have run for my life. He said nothing. It was like being in a fairground sideshow where you drop a quarter in a machine, punch a button, and a freak is supposed to start talking. I turned and left for the other side of the cellblock where people were pleasant. Very strange — my thinking a section of death row was pleasant.

When we got to the lobby that divides the two sides, Ron told me about his conversation with Bryant, who had no remorse for anything he had done, and he even laughed about his crimes. He told Ron that his own mother shot him in the side when he was a child, and that he had been abused throughout his life.

It's no wonder in my mind he is serving 115 years, two life sentences, and one death sentence on the row. I'll use a baseball metaphor to explain. Some of us are born on third base, and all we need is a teammate to get a hit and we'll be home free. Others have to pick up a bat, step up to the plate, and score on their own. A few, like Stephen Bryant, are born in the dugout, and they never make it into the batter's box. They never get a chance to prove themselves.

I took a left, walked upstairs, and stopped at the first cell, where an older man named Donald lived. He jumped up off his bed and headed my way. I thought about my dog that used to leap off the couch and ran, tail wagging, to me when I got home.

Donald wiped his hands on his shirt and reached out with his right one to shake mine. I thought about the first time that happened to me on death row — when the inmate said he only shakes with his left hand and so on and so forth. Gross. But I shook Donald's right hand anyway. I was speechless for a while thinking about why he wiped it on his shirt. I moved on down the line to Michigander Richard Moore's cell. He was eating at his desk, which was not unusual. He stood up rather gingerly.

"What's wrong?" I asked.

"I have a cyst in the middle of my back and it hurts. Having surgery on it soon. They're going to cut it out. Medical has popped it twice, but it keeps filling back up with liquid, so they're going to remove it."

"Where will you go?" I asked.

"We have medical people here but for surgery, we go to Columbia. The prison there has a hospital in it."

"What's that process like?"

"It sucks," Richard said. "They drive us in a van that has two armed officers in it. There's another van in front of us and an unmarked car behind us. In all, there are five officers that transfer people on death row. Ridiculous."

"Do you have the right to get routine checkups?"

"Yes, but you need to request them," he said. "They won't tell you when it's time for something to be done. I had a colonoscopy not long ago because I'm at the age that I need one. I had to ask for it. I was transferred to Columbia and they did it there. After it was done, they told me that my intestine was twisted or something like that, and the procedure didn't work. They told me I had to reschedule for another time. So, about four weeks later, a guard showed up here and told me that I was going for a ride that day. Didn't tell me where. They put me in the van and took me to Columbia again. I figured I was getting another colonoscopy, but when the doctor came in, he said my procedure was rescheduled and told me the date. They took me all the way up there just to tell me it had been rescheduled! I was pissed."

"Seems like you would enjoy getting out of your cell for the day and going for a ride. No?" I asked.

"Yeah, if it's a short ride, but not all the way to Columbia. They handcuff us, and put a black box on the cuffs between our hands so we can't move them from side to side or up and down. We have a belly chain, which is connected to the cuffs. Hands are strapped to that chain right up against our stomach. And they put leg chains on us."

He demonstrated all of this to me — stuck his hands out of his cell so I could see the cuff marks on his wrists.

"It's a very, very painful ride," Richard continued. "That's why I was pissed off when they brought me all the way up there to tell me that. You should also be pissed — it took five officers and all that gas in the cars to do that. That's your tax money," adding he wasn't mad at the officers who transported him. "They're just doing their job. It's not their fault."

Our conversation turned to the public perception of death row.

"Most people think death row is a dangerous place and that there are a lot of fights in here," I said.

"Of course they do, because that's what they're told. We get this television channel here that shows those lockup shows. Do you watch them?"

"All the time."

"I've never seen any death row footage on those shows, but I did see a red "Death Row" sign. That makes people think that we're all violent and causing trouble, but it ain't us on that show. It's the general population. It's the same with the news around here. When they report an incident here, they always say that Lieber is where all of South Carolina's death row inmates are housed, and then they show that red sign. Instantly, everyone thinks that whatever incident they're reporting on happened in here … There's nothing we can do about it … We're all serving a death sentence in this world. Everyone on this planet is serving a death sentence, not just us."

"I tell people how quiet it is in here. I tell them that you guys couldn't hurt each other if you wanted to," I said.

He looked at me, rolled his eyes, and smirked. The guy in the cell next to Richard — his "neighbor" — heard us talking and listened in as always. His name is Luzenski Cottrell. He is on the row for killing a Myrtle Beach police officer. In total, he's serving 30 years plus one life sentence and one death sentence. He didn't say much, but I knew he was paying attention. When I made that last comment, he laughed. I took that to mean that they do have the opportunity to hurt each other. I don't know how they could do that, but Moore's smirk and Cottrell's laughter told me that there's a way.

I told them that people are very curious about life on death row: "People are interested in learning about things they can't relate to. Death row is a hidden world and you'd be surprised at how intrigued people are by it."

Cottrell: "You're right, man! Check this out. I have a pen pal in

England and he said the same thing." He slid a letter through the bars of his cell for me to look at. "Read the last sentence."

Me (reading it out loud): "For one reason or another, everyone I talk to is so fascinated by American death row."

I thanked Moore and Cottrell, and I said it was time for me to move on.

"Thanks for coming in," Richard said. "Keep teaching those kids."

A few cells down to the right is where Stephen Stanko lives. I walked down and looked in. He sat at his desk writing as usual.

"Mr. Stanko. How are you, sir?"

He peered over his right shoulder. "Hey, Principal!" he said then stood, took off his glasses and walked toward me. "How's the book coming?"

I had not told him I was writing a book but did express interest in it to him. It was the first thing he asked me about ever since. I said I was having a hard time with structure and format; that I knew what I wanted to say, but struggled with the sequence and details. I didn't want to bore my readers.

Stanko: "You and Ron are polar opposites — different in almost every way: intellectually, emotionally, everything. I don't know anything about your upbringing, but you're an educator, so I assume you had a good childhood. And Ron's a felon. But here you are, walking into death row together, voluntarily helping people — helping us. That's very interesting. Everyone has a book in them, but only one in a thousand will be a bestseller. You have a bestseller and all you have to do is write it. If you want me to help, just ask. I don't want anything — except the truth. Truth is stranger than fiction. There are books out there about death row, but they're fiction. Get the truth out and you'll be set."

Stanko told me about a law professor who asked him to address his students on the subject of criminal justice. "He knew that I had talked to college classes before via phone," Stanko said about the professor. "I never offer that, but if people ask, I always say yes. I spent 90 minutes on the phone with his class and got some familiar questions: 'What's your day-to-day life like? How do inmates treat each other? What's it like contemplating the day you'll be executed?'"

Stanko said inmates only get 15 minutes per call, so they have to call right back, get another 15 minutes and so on and so forth. For this particular class, it was a 90-minute conversation, so Stanko had to call back six times.

"A couple weeks later, the professor came back in to thank me," Stanko continued. "He said his students got a lot out of that conversation, and it was something they would never forget. But, he said, 'I never tell them how calm and nice you guys are in here.' That offended me greatly."

"Did you ask him about it?" I asked Stanko.

"He just shrugged his shoulders — pretending to be a tough guy ... coming in here and facing us ... I told him there was nothing stopping me from reaching through these bars and pulling him against this door if I wanted to. I choose not to, though. That's what I mean about telling the truth. He left out a huge part of what this place is. We're not violent. Sure, there are people in here who make bad decisions, and there have been times when certain people try to harm the guards, but he's never seen that. Tell people what you see and tell the truth. That's what I mean by truth is stranger than fiction. Don't feed the public's false perception. I doubt he'll ever come back in here, but if he does, I ain't helping him again, that's for sure."

"I tell people all the time how quiet and relatively peaceful it is on death row," I said. "I've never seen problems with the guards or anything, although I'm sure it exists."

Stanko (laughing): "I'm glad you didn't stop in yesterday!"

"What happened?"

"I'd been having a problem with my sink for a couple days. The drain wasn't working, and nobody would come and fix it. Finally, a plumber arrived, but he wasn't a real plumber. He was an ex-correctional officer who used to work here. I knew him. I told him what was going on, and he could tell I was upset. He puffed out his chest and told me to settle down in a condescending tone.

"That's when I lost my temper. Water flooded my cell and I was afraid my papers would get wet. He fixed the leak but I was still angry. If my papers got wet, I would have really lost it on this guy! He did fix it, but I was pretty angry."

We talked about William Bell, the inmate I spent a lot of time talking to last time I was there. He's the one who told me he is on death row for his role in killing a school principal.

"He didn't react at all to me telling him what I do for a living," I said. "I was surprised by that. I guess he didn't see the irony like I did."

Stanko: (smirking) "Oh, he did. Trust me. You didn't get the reaction you expected because, you have to remember, he's served almost 30 years in here. He's been conditioned to not show emotion — almost 30 years. His exterior wall is thick. I wasn't sure how much he shared with you about his case. Now that I know you know the details, I'm going to talk to him about you next time I see him out at rec."

I could hear that Stanko's radio was playing sports talk. I knew he was a University of South Carolina Gamecocks fan — it was obvious with the stickers on his door.

"What are you listening to? Sounds like sports talk."

Stanko: "Yeah, I'm getting ready to listen to the baseball game. The Gamecocks play tonight. They just beat Clemson two out of three last week. They should have lost one of those games, but somehow pulled it off. Is Michigan any good at baseball?"

Me: "Not as good as teams down South."

Stanko: "They have a pretty good basketball team. South Carolina beat them earlier this year, though! Frank Martin had that team playing pretty good, but they've lost a few recently. I'm hoping they can make a run in the tournament. I'll be listening in."

It was about 6:30 p.m. and I was ready to get out of there. I never knew exactly what time it was because they made me take off my watch going in. Ron was downstairs talking to William Bell — the inmate who killed the school principal — and I walked down there to let him know it was time to go. Visitors must be off the premises at 7 p.m.. When I approached them, William stuck his hand out to shake mine.

"Steve. Good to see you," he said.

"Mr. Bell. Good to see you, too."

"I know you guys have to go, but I need to tell you something," Bell said. "When you left last time, I sat on my bed and thought about you for a long time. I was scratching my head all night."

"I'm surprised to hear that," I said. "After you told me why you were in here and then I told you what I do for a living, you barely reacted at all."

"Because I was so shocked! I didn't know what to say. I still can't believe it. I'm a firm believer that everything happens for a reason, but I can't figure out how to process this. Why did we meet?" he asked.

"I'm not sure, but I'm glad to hear you thought it was as shocking as I did. It gave me goosebumps when you were telling your story. I've shared it with a lot of people, and they all think it's as crazy as I do."

"Yeah, man. It's pretty remarkable," he said.

I was relieved that he thought about it as much as I did. It told me that he felt remorse. Of all the professions in this world, what are the chances of him meeting me on death row? I'm sure our meeting brought him right back to that night.

"Alright Mr. Bell, I need to get going. You need to get to bed. Two a.m. is going to come quickly and you need to get your rest before doing those 200 burpees, 300 push-ups, and 200 bucket-of-water curls," I said.

William (laughing): "You got that right! See you next time."

Chapter 8

I knew my sixth trip to Lieber would be my last inside Hell's waiting room. I had learned a lot about the row and thought I'd given something back to the inmates as well. Most of us want to live a good and useful life. Of course, whether each of us is doing so or not is debatable, but one thing for sure is the overwhelming majority of us, including me, have better lives than the 37 men living out their days on South Carolina's death row.

If you think your life isn't as good as others, you have a problem. Perhaps you spend too much time on social media or never leave your house or whatever. Fact is, foolish comparison of yourself to others is the thief of joy. Clear your mind and visit the residents of death row and you will walk out with a brand spanking new perspective. The most surprising thing for me was the degree of positivity and hope in the voices of many of them. If they can do this then you and I have no excuse for getting down in the dumps.

Death row is the dumps, and it's reassuring to know they'll never get out and do us harm. It's comforting to know that we are not them. Yet we seem to enjoy reading about monsters and seeing their faces on a television screen provided they remain detained behind bars. We know we're not supposed to glorify these killers — especially in public or perhaps in the movies long after they're dead.

But it's important to understand who they are, what they think, and what they do with what's left of their lives. I've been there. I talked to them face to face. I was frightened at first but after a while most of what seemed surreal became strangely comfortable. Truth really is stranger than fiction. There's really nothing comparable to listening to someone explain how they "justifiably" killed two police officers.

Anyway, on my final visit to the prison I noted that 1,206 inmates were incarcerated there that day and returned to the right-hand side of death row. I started at the floor level and worked my way around the perimeter until I reached the cell of William Bell. His overhead light was off at first but when I peered through the window, he looked up at me and flipped the switch. He walked to the front of his cell and extended his right hand. We shook hands and we talked.

"If there was one thing you could tell the outside world, what would it be?" I asked.

"I would tell them that nobody is born a killer — that's a learned behavior. Society plays a huge role in developing killers, and I'm living proof. We need to reach troubled kids before they get to high school. Afterwards is too late. They've already made hard choices and know the difference between right and wrong. We should start with them at least by elementary school. That's your homework, Steve."

We laughed and I agreed, then asked if there was any news about when he would return to the prison's general population. He said he hoped he'd be moved summer's end. "Over the past 29 years, several people in here got their cases overturned. It's amazing. They walk taller, talk differently, their personalities change. I was happy for them, but could not help wondering if it would happen to me. After 25 years, I had almost lost all hope. It was on my last appeal when I got a call. I was on that phone right there (pointing to the pay phone on wheels not far away). I was standing where I am right now. I picked up the phone and heard my whole team of lawyers on the other end. I'll never forget the exact words I heard that day: 'Mr. Bell, the judge ruled in your favor.'

"I immediately thought of my mother. She had passed away. But I knew she was smiling down on me. Then, I cried. Shortly afterward, I thought about the guys I'd be leaving. They're all I've had for the past 29 years of my life. I will miss them."

I was surprised to hear him say this. He had just received the best news of his life, and among his first thoughts was how much he would miss the murderers who surrounded him. It reminded me of his humanity, of his ability to have real human relationships and to express real human emotions.

I wondered about how the appeals process worked in a death sentence case, and asked him to explain.

"After being sentenced to die, the first appeal is directly to the South Carolina Supreme Court. If it is denied, the next one is to the US Supreme Court. If that's denied, the appeal goes to PCR (post-conviction relief). Next, it is taken up in (US) District Court. After that, it's back to the state Supreme Court. If denied again, it goes to the 4th (US) Circuit Court of Appeals. The last chance is the South Carolina Supreme Court again. If you see the South Carolina Supreme Court three times, you're out. That's where I was when, finally, I got a ruling in my favor. It took 28 years."

He talked a little about the Antiterrorism and Effective Death Penalty Act that President Clinton signed in 1996. It was supposed to speed up the process, but didn't. He also said South Carolina legalized lethal injections in 1994 as a means for execution, and four inmates immediately dropped their appeals. In his words, they "checked out."

"Why would they do that?" I asked.

"Before lethal injection, it was only the chair. Lethal injection was supposed to be a peaceful way to go … It's not such a peaceful death though… Lots of pain and suffering is involved, but it's not so obvious because the body is paralyzed and you can't move."

A death row inmate in the United States waits on average 15 years between sentencing and execution. Nothing is fast with our legal system, even with the so-called Effective Death Penalty Act. Because of delay built into that law, 25 percent of death row inmates die of natural causes while awaiting execution. Also notable is the cost of incarceration of death row inmates. Each one costs taxpayers about $90,000 more per year than a prisoner in the general population. Multiply that by 29 years.

As William Bell and I discussed all this that day, dinner was served from the wheeled cart by a corrections officer. The food was boxed but certainly not "to go." All were dine-in customers for sure. Bell accepted his but his neighbor to the left asked the officer to give his to inmate Northcutt along with a pack of chocolate Nutter Butter crackers. I guess it was Northcutt's lucky day.

"I hear a lot about the racial divide in prisons. Do you feel that you get treated differently here because you're black?" I asked Bell.

"No. There are some that will stick their chests out and portray the tough-guy image, but that's not because I'm black. Most of them are respectful. Wouldn't you be? They have to deal with us every day. There have been white supremacists back here, though. They put up stickers on their cells that say, "Preserve the white race." They don't say much, though, because they know they're outnumbered. I don't take it personally anyway because I know that's how they were raised. I was raised around drugs, guns, and violence and they were raised to be white supremacists. I stay away from them."

Bell then recommended a book titled *Slavery by Another Name*. "Read it; you'll learn a lot."

I also mentioned to him that I was not allowed inside Lieber's maximum-security block, which is next to death row. "Why do you think that is?" I asked.

"They're nuts in there. You don't want to go inside. Not safe."

I thanked him for telling me his story and said I had to go. I suspect he knew I wouldn't return. But I didn't tell him that and he didn't ask. I walked up the stairs and saw Fred Singleton standing close to his door, peering out at me. He's a 74-year-old African-American who has been on death row since 1983. He is serving 137 years for armed robbery, burglary, larceny, grand larceny, first-degree criminal sexual conduct, and escape. He also has a death sentence for murder. Singleton is South Carolina's longest tenured death row inmate. He got there the year I was born.

He won't be executed until he is declared mentally fit to participate in his sentencing trial, and from my brief interactions with him, I don't think it will happen anytime soon. He seems like a nice guy, but what he says makes very little sense. We spoke briefly and I moved on down to Stanko's cell.

"What's one thing you want people on the outside to know?" I asked Stanko.

Stanko (after about 10 seconds): "Don't make your judgment about me from one moment in time."

I thought, "You had more than one moment, buddy," but said nothing.

Stanko: "The people who you think are the worst of the worst, aren't. Things aren't as bad as you think they are. That's a good life lesson for any situation, not just ours back here."

I think he was referring to the public's perception of death row. We tend to think it's a horrible place, which it is, but the inmates are neither pitching fits nor causing problems. Most seemed to be rather peaceful, hopeful human beings. I think that's what Stanko was trying to tell me. But there are more than 2,500 people living on death rows in the United States, so my sample size is very low.

Stanko had been critical about his treatment, so I prodded a bit.

"You have voiced concerns about the guards to me in past conversations. What is your overall feeling about how they treat you?" I asked him.

Stanko: "It's all about respect. If they respect me and listen to me, I'll do the same. I'm not an animal but I am in a cage, so don't poke me!"

I had been around Stanko long enough to know that his demeanor was generally calm and engaging, but that it could quickly change. I would not want to get on his bad side.

Stanko continued: "Some people, officers included, come in here with an agenda. We can tell. If we thought you had an agenda, Steve, nobody would talk to you. You've gotten a lot of people to talk, so that's a good reflection on your character."

I took that as a compliment but remained wary — like I am around people who have snakes for pets.

As I was leaving that day I thought about the fact that those men would not be executed by drugs if they dropped all further appeals. That's because no deadly drugs are being made available by manufacturers, which don't produce them because they don't want to tarnish their reputations. I also considered the fact that no one on death row would be electrocuted unless he agreed to die that way because the state no longer mandates it. I wondered what the families of the victims thought about it.

On top of that, there is the strong possibility a few of those men are innocent of the crime for which they are scheduled to be executed by the state. Odds are at least three of those 37 condemned men are innocent. Human error happens everywhere, and death row is no exception.

Chapter 9

Soon after my last visit to death row on March 29, 2017, I was contacted by a news editor at the *Post and Courier* in Charleston. Since reporters are not allowed inside the prison walls, let alone death row, to interview prisoners, the editor asked if I would allow someone from the newspaper to interview me for a story on what I had experienced at Lieber. The prison probably would not like me talking to the newspaper very much.

If I did the interview, I knew that more than likely I would no longer be allowed back inside the place. I was also certain that many of the inmates looked forward to seeing me, enjoyed talking to someone like me from the outside. One reason I started visiting death row was to try and help them in some way. I was also curious about who they were and how they lived. By the time the newspaper contacted me, I had satisfied those intentions.

By then I had developed an odd feeling about being too comfortable during my visits. I was no longer nervous, frightened, or even on edge in that place, all of which I concluded was not healthy. Yet I remained careful while on the inside and was very much aware of the surroundings. As I said, it was an odd feeling.

Initially I was reluctant to speak to a reporter because I might let the inmates down. Sounds crazy, I know. I sensed I might have been the only person who ever interacted with the men without expecting anything in return other than interesting conversation. They get visits from lawyers and members of the clergy. Some have family members who come to see them. But I was different. I wondered if they would miss me, and have since concluded that they do to some degree.

I struggled with doing the interview. I reminded myself that they were very dangerous people who had committed very heinous crimes. And I could never put out of my mind what I thought were the feelings of their victims' loved ones, especially what they would think if they read about my interactions with people who had caused them much pain and anguish.

I agreed to do the interview — and to subsequently write this book — because people should know what death row is like. My goal was – and remains – to give an honest account of the physical environment as well as what I considered to be the general mental state of the men South Carolina has condemned to die in the name of each and every one of its citizens. I agreed to share my story in the hope that it would encourage others to volunteer their time to help those condemned men in some way. I especially wanted everyone to know that I never felt that my life was in danger while there. I didn't see or hear any fights, and the guards and prisoners treated each other with respect. I know that awful things happen in prisons, but I did not experience any of it.

Television makes it seem as if death row is a loud, violent, and terrible place. I'll give them terrible, but not violent and loud — not while I was there. We hear so many negative stories about prisons. I felt that mine should focus on the human side of it — to be a breath of fresh air, if you will.

So I agreed to do the interview. "You probably won't be allowed back in that prison if we run this story," the editor said. "You know that, right?"

I assured him that I was OK with it, and soon met with the reporter. She asked a lot of good questions and we talked for a long time about my experiences and my feelings. "You were allowed to walk right up to their cells? You didn't have to talk to them behind the plexiglass? Explain to me again how you were allowed back there in the first place."

On Sunday, June 4, 2017, the story ran on the front page of the *Post and Courier*. It read in part:

Steven Schonveld didn't know whether to call it coincidental or crazy, but the goosebumps up and down his body told him his conversation with a convicted killer had struck a nerve.

It was a winter afternoon during one of Schonveld's visits to death row at Lieber Correctional Institution. Several times since September, the 34-year-old assistant principal drove from his job at Orange Grove Charter School in Charleston to the Ridgeville prison. His goal? To have 'normal' conversations with those facing the harshest punishment for what are classified as some of the most heinous crimes in the state.

He found himself standing before the cell of William Bell, a 48-year-old man serving two death sentences for the armed robbery and slaying of an elementary school principal in Anderson. Bell leaned against his cell and spoke slowly and deliberately.

The killing happened late one night in 1988 as he and two buddies walked through a school parking lot. They robbed the principal of his wallet and shot him twice — once in the back and once in the head — as the man walked to his car. Bell, unaware when recounting his story that Schonveld was an educator, said they killed the principal because he'd seen their faces and could identify them. They weren't thinking about the death penalty at the time …

Taken aback, he told Bell: "I am an assistant principal of an elementary school. I walk to my car in the dark at night often. What you just described hits really close to home." Later, reflecting on the conversation, Schonveld wrote:

"Out of all the professionals in this world, what are the chances of him meeting someone inside death row that was basically the same person whom his crime was against? I'm sure our meeting brought him right back to that night."

Access to death row isn't easy to come by. Reporters can't get in. Relatives and other visitors are allowed, but Plexiglas separates them from the inmates. Schonveld, however, was able to approach their cells, getting a glimpse of how men live out their lives when they're waiting to die. He brought a notebook to document what he heard, and he wrote his reflections in a journal after each visit …

Schonveld returned to death row five times … his last visit to death row was in March. His goal was to gain perspective, and he thinks he's accomplished that. He's shared his writings with friends and colleagues. He wanted people who will never set foot inside death row to take away that the inmates have done horrible things but "they're still human beings …"

Robert Dunham, executive director of the Death Penalty Information Center in Washington, D.C., cautioned against drawing too many broad conclusions from Schonveld's experience as each death row has a different culture and impressions can vary depending on which inmates a visitor is exposed to. Some 2,902 people are awaiting execution in the nation's prisons.

In general, Dunham said, how well inmates fare on death row often depends on factors such as the amount of solitary confinement to which they're exposed and the degree of humanity with which they are treated. Solitary confinement can be psychologically debilitating and it's not uncommon for death row inmates to struggle with mental illnesses, emotional impairments and cognitive disorders, he said.

"How they perceive life on death row and the future is often filtered through these lenses," he said.

As for Schonveld, he went in without a firm opinion on capital punishment. Now, weighing the costs and the delays involved with executions, he wonders what the point is. He also struggles with the question of what makes one murder worse than another.

"They've all committed terrible, terrible crimes, and you could argue that they all deserve to be there. I just don't see it working. I don't know what the goal is," he said ...

In the hours and days following the article, I got a lot of calls, texts, and messages. Almost all of them were positive. My favorite reaction was from a colleague at work who walked into my office with the paper in her hand and said, "I had no idea you were so interesting!" I laughed and responded with the only thing I could think of, "Well, now you do!"

I even got some reactions from some of my middle school students. Their parents let them read the article and they came to school telling me that they enjoyed it. I thought that was really cool. I felt upbeat and energetic about how it turned out and the reactions I was getting from it. Not everyone, however, saw it as a good thing.

Chapter 10

On June 7, 2017, a few days after the article was published in the *Post and Courier*, I received an email from a woman named Diana Holt. It read:

Subject: Death row intrusion

Mr. Schonveld-

I write on behalf of the lawyers whose death row clients were victims of your inappropriate communications with them. I would like to speak with you concerning this. Please advise when you and I can share a phone call. Thank you.

Regards~dh

That subject line set the tone. Ms. Holt might be the first person in the history of the world to refer to someone on death row as a victim of "inappropriateness." None of my communications were inappropriate. I went in with an open mind. I didn't judge the inmates. I didn't put words into their mouths. I didn't make up anything. I did not force them to talk to me — which would have been impossible.

I was allowed into the maximum-security prison on six occasions. If anyone thought I was communicating inappropriately, surely the authorities would have stopped me from returning. They would have halted me at the door, offered me some sort of orientation, or advised me on what I could and could not say or do. Nobody questioned me. Not once did anyone ask about my intentions other than what was on my application for volunteer services, which was approved. The only question came from the officers at the front gate:

"Where are you going?"

"Death row," I said.

On six occasions I parked my car, walked into the prison through various security checkpoints, through additional gates and into the maximum security building, past the holding cells, down the corridors and by the kitchen into death row, where I was patted down before the final gate opened into the belly of the beast. No one asked me why I was there or what I was talking to the offenders about. The only people at Lieber who asked about my presence were the individuals who lived there. My answer was always the same: I was curious and I wanted to help.

I understand why Ms. Holt was concerned. She was part of a group of lawyers that represents some of the inmates. Lawyers do not want their clients speaking about their crimes to anyone else, especially if it might jeopardize their appeals. I get that. But anyone with a reliable internet connection could look up any prisoner — not just on death row — anywhere in the state prison system. It's not hard to find out where they are, what their convictions are, what their sentences are, and a lot of other things about them. It's a matter of public record. And anyone can write them a letter.

To get information about their cases, simply type in their name into the search bar at the top of the computer screen and press Enter. To get information on an inmate who happens to be on death row, it helps to put a comma after the name and the words "death row" afterward.

That's what I did, and I got a list of articles about each one — their crimes, stories in newspapers, and court documents. I clicked on the images tab, and saw their photos. Their convictions are not private. Their criminal histories are not private. Their conduct in prison is not private. Their addresses are not private.

Ms. Holt, the defense lawyer, was upset, but she should have expressed her concerns to authorities at the Department of Corrections, not me. Perhaps she did. I don't know. I did not respond directly to her. I called Lieber and asked to speak to the warden, who I had met in the prison yard. When I spoke to him on the phone, I told him who I was and asked if he read the newspaper article.

"Yes, I did," he said.

"What did you think?"

He said he didn't have a problem with the article itself, adding that it did create some problems within the department.

"How so?"

He said he was asked how I got access to death row.

I explained that I followed every procedure, filled out the application for volunteer services, and was approved. I told him that it was my hope that the article would open the eyes of others who were thinking about volunteering to help in the Department of Corrections, and hoped more volunteers would come in as a result.

"We aren't allowing any volunteers in here anymore right now," he said.

"Until when?"

"Indefinitely," he said, "and when we do open volunteer services back up, everyone will have to reapply."

"So I will need to submit my application again?"

"I wouldn't waste your time," he said.

Message received. He also said the prison system was fortunate it was me that got in and not someone else. I apologized for any trouble I had caused him and said I was surprised volunteer services were shut down because of me. I told him what happened was the opposite of what I had hoped would come from the article.

I was later forwarded an email from Ron that said any volunteer at Lieber who had not been through an orientation at the prison but wished to stay on the volunteer list had to attend an upcoming class, and that it applied to all state prisons, not just Lieber. I did not get that email directly. They forgot to send it to me, right? While I'm happy that volunteers can get back in, I'm certain my presence is not desired.

I've received numerous questions and comments from people about my experience. Most asked if I still go in and if I would like to return. But I have heard nothing from any of the men on death row. I wonder if they read the article? They did have access to the *Post and Courier*. I pictured them passing it around on the rolling cart from one cell to the next. "Article in the paper about us! Coming down!"

But during one of our talks, Stanko said, "So if you're ever not allowed back, feel free to write me. I get a lot of letters. I'll write you back." So on August 8, 2017, two months after the article was published, I wrote to him:

Mr. Stanko,

This is Steve Schonveld, Assistant Principal at Orange Grove. I am writing you because I am curious about several things and it's become clear that I will likely never be allowed back in the prison to talk to you in person again. I trust that you read the article that was in the Post and Courier on June 4th about my visits and Ron. I took to heart what you told me about making sure I tell the truth about what I observed in death row. Everything I said was 100% truth, with some of my reflections mixed in, of course. I thought the article was written well and the public seemed to have a lot of interest in it. I've gotten a lot of feedback and questions from it…good and bad. What were your thoughts about it? Was there anything in it that you wish wasn't printed?

I know there have been some changes in the prison since then. I've heard that visitors are not permitted in death row anymore. Is that true? If so, I think that's a huge mistake. My intention was to have the exact opposite effect, as a matter of fact. I was hoping it would open the eyes of more people, which would encourage more visitors. Unfortunately, the prison didn't seem to see it that way. I get the feeling that any press is bad press for them. Death row seems to be a secret that the state wants to keep quiet.

I read last week that there is a new warden in charge now. I know there was a well-publicized escape on July 4th, but I don't know if that played a role in the change of leadership. Ron and I hope that we didn't have anything to do with the change.

Please tell Johnny Bennett and Richard Moore that I say hello. If I recall correctly, I don't believe you're on the same side as Marion Lindsey, but if you have any contact with him, please tell him I say hello as well…he and I had some good conversations. I know Bell is off death row. I was very happy to see that and I know he's thrilled. That's good lawyer work right there!

How are your writings coming along? What are you working on now?

I hope you are doing well and I look forward to hearing back from you soon. You can send a reply to:

(address redacted)

About a week later I got an email from Mark Peper, a local lawyer and friend who had spoken to Ms. Holt on the phone. She had contacted him via email:

Subject: Schonveld Letter

Mark ~

Are you representing Mr. Schonveld or no? I would have thought you would have instructed him not to contact death row inmates that he libeled in his article for *the Post and Courier*, as I requested. We have obtained all of his written communications with SCDC and know that he misrepresented his intentions. Do we need to sue? Just say.

Best~ dh

Attached to her email was the letter I wrote to Stanko. She copied a lot of people on this email as well. I didn't know who they were.

Here is Peper's reply:

Subject: RE: Schonveld Letter

Representing him for what, exactly? As a fellow SCACDL member who's familiar and appreciative of the work you and your counterparts do, I'm still confused as to how your clients can be damaged by receiving a compassionate letter from a middle school vice principal. Perhaps Mr. Schonveld would relate better to being courteously informed as to how his contact with an inmate could be detrimental to their past, present, or future legal posture, as opposed to being attacked and threatened to be sued. Just a thought, since we're all on the same team here.

On a side note, and contrary to your assertion below, Steve has assured me that this was his one and only written communication with SCDC and further assured me it will be his last, especially now that he knows it won't make it to the intended recipient.

Best,

Mark

She was upset that I would write Stanko a letter and again threatened to sue me. I can write a letter to anyone I want to. Ms. Holt told Mark that she has all of the written communications that I have sent to the prison. Great, so she has one letter. I have written exactly one letter.

Shortly after that email exchange, I received a letter in the mail at work. The envelope was from "Justice 360 – Advanced Equality in Capital Cases":

Dear Mr. Schonveld,

My client, Stephen Stanko, forwarded me your letter to him dated August 8, 2017. At his request, I respectfully ask you do not attempt to contact him again.

I also represent Johnny Bennett, Richard Moore, and William Bell. Please do not make any attempts to contact them. Any contact with my clients should be made through me.

Thank you for your cooperation.

Kind Regards,

Lindsey S. Vann

I considered Ms. Vann's letter a much better way of communicating than threatening a lawsuit. But I don't think Stanko ever saw my letter. I don't think he would have read my letter and not responded. If he didn't want me writing him, he would have written back saying so. He would not have ignored me.

That was my one and only attempt at writing a letter to an inmate. I was hoping to keep the lines of communication open, but it became clear that was not going to be the case. A little more than a month later, I read a newspaper article that the state transferred all 37 death row inmates in an overnight operation from Lieber, where they had been for 20 years, to Kirkland Correctional Institution in Columbia. Staff shortages at Lieber were cited as the main reason for the relocation. It said the change was also done to put the inmates closer to the state's mental health care facilities and appellate courts, cutting down on time-consuming transfers.

Part of me thinks those lawyers played a part in getting their clients out of Lieber. Perhaps the warden did not want to have to deal with it. Or maybe he did. But it's good to know that people on death row have lawyers who care about their clients. Family and friends might give up on them, but legal counsel apparently will not. Fact is, our justice system allows for appeals regardless of the sentence, and some death row inmates do get out in ways other than a casket. Some have had their sentences reduced to life in prison and others have walked out as free men.

Justice 360 is an exceptional nonprofit organization doing amazing things for capital punishment cases. I respect the work they do and wish them continued success. Convictions are reversible. Execution is not.

Chapter 11

"What do you think the difference is between people who end up on death row and people who don't?"

This was one of the questions I asked some of the inmates on my final visit to Lieber. One of them cocked his head to the side a little and said:

"It's like checkers and chess. When you play checkers, you're reacting to your opponent's move and not thinking much about what you're going to do next. You make a move, he makes a move, you make a move, he makes a move, until someone screws up and the game is over. … Chess is another story. Each piece has a different role. You have to think about the result of your move a lot more before you make it. There's a lot of strategy and planning involved. I grew up playing checkers with my life when I should have been playing chess."

I've shared that analysis with my students because I know they can relate to it. Our society is focused on getting results fast. When a teacher questions a student, an instant answer is usually expected, and most of the time that's what the teacher gets. Consequently, students can be extremely frustrated when they come up short. I see this often. We live in a reactive society that could benefit by practicing more patience. The process of reasoning takes time.

The death penalty is such a hotly debated issue in part because it takes time and effort to understand all that is at stake. No matter how obvious it is that someone is guilty, he or she is entitled to appeal the verdict. The level of frustration and anger associated with this is almost unbearable for the families of the victims as well as the accused. But it's important to remember that 60 percent of all death sentences in South Carolina have been reversed on appeals.

Meanwhile, the victims' family and friends are on a roller coaster of emotions:

— He's going to die for his crime. I don't need to worry one more second about him.

— He's not going to die for this crime, but he's going to spend the rest of his life in prison.

— He's up for parole next year? I'll have to go to the hearing and relive the whole thing as I try to convince the parole board not to let him out.

— He's out! Where is he? What's he doing? Am I or my family in danger?

The general public doesn't know what happens behind the prison gates, especially on death row. Taxpayers spend a lot of money on prisons but aren't allowed inside, especially on the row. What the public does know typically comes from people who work inside the prison system, thus the information is often one-sided. That's not good when trying to understand what the criminal justice system is all about.

Citizens should know exactly what they are paying for; this applies not only to the criminal justice system, but also public schools, public highways and transportation, law enforcement, and so on.

When considering the value of the death penalty, I wonder if society is better off after the accused has been executed? I also ask, as a productive member of the community, do I feel safer knowing this person is dead or is it enough to know he is locked away where he poses no threat to law-abiding citizens?

An eye for an eye is the response I get most often when discussing the death penalty with its supporters. I understand that. I can't help but wonder if it is about revenge or justice. What we are supposed to have in the United States is a system of justice, not a system of revenge. Perhaps keeping a killer alive in a cage is worse than death.

Redemption is impossible after the killer is put to death. Can we have the death penalty and believe that everyone is capable of redeeming themselves? Maybe some people are capable of redemption and others are too far gone. If everyone is capable of redemption, how long must one wait? Is there a time limit on redeeming yourself? Are these the worst humans on the planet or are they just the humans who have made the worst decisions? Is it who they are or simply what they did? Is there a difference?

Several of the men on death row said they hoped others would not judge them solely on the crime that landed them there. Am I so focused on the punishment that I can't see the man without seeing his crime? That was and still is a huge hurdle for me when considering the matter. I think most people are better than what they do at their worst moments, and I feel that way about most of the men I got to know on death row.

What's the worst thing you've done in your life? Not the worst thing you've been caught doing, but what you have done. Pretend for a moment that the worst thing you have ever done was to drive drunk. That's something a lot of people can relate to. Many of us have gotten behind the wheel of a car when we know we shouldn't have. The worst possible outcome of that decision is killing someone else, yourself, or both. You set your own self up to commit a horrible crime. You're driving down the road, intoxicated, and you get in an accident. You were only going four miles per hour over the speed limit, but the driver of the car that you cut off swerved to avoid you and hit a tree. She was ejected from the car and died from her injuries. Now, you face the very serious charge of involuntary manslaughter or possibly second-degree murder. You've never committed a crime before in your life and you just received a sentence of 10 years in prison. You are a murderer.

Would you want that moment to define you? Of course not. You're better than that. You're better than the worst thing you've ever done. We all are. We've all done things we're not proud of. Things we regret. Things we wish we'd have done differently. Nobody wants their entire existence judged by that unfortunate incident.

Most of the men I met on death row asked that I see them as more than convicted killers. So I got to know them as best I could. I looked them in the eyes. I shook their murderous hands. I listened. They seemed to be at peace with themselves — as if they had grieved their own deaths while still alive in their cells. For some, there wasn't anything left to be angry about other than not getting a shower when they wanted one, or that the plumbing wasn't working properly. The small things become the big things. Think about how flustered you might get if your morning routine is interrupted — when you don't get your morning cup of joe.

Humans change. We learn things and we typically are better people as a result. Some of us have learned that it's not wise to paint ourselves into corners when discussing important issues. I've been to death row. I have learned things. I have changed.

Why do some murderers get the death penalty, some get life in prison without the possibility of parole, and others get 30 years or less with a chance of early release? Approximately 13 percent (180,000 out of about 1,316,000) of all inmates in US prisons are killers. There are certain criteria that a crime must meet to be deemed eligible for the death penalty. Although rules differ from state to state, capital conviction in this nation means murder involving one or more of the following factors:

— Victim is a police officer, firefighter, paramedic, or similar public safety professional.

— Victim is killed during the commission of another violent felony (often called felony murder).

— Victim is tortured, raped, or sexually assaulted, particularly if the victim is a child.

— Multiple murders were committed.

— It was a murder-for-hire.

— It was an act of terrorism.

While those criteria fit most people's definitions of a worst-case scenario, they do raise red flags. If a loved one is murdered but the case does not meet the criteria, the killer would not face the death penalty. That means the justice system does not value some loved one's lives as much as those of someone else. Same crime; same result; different punishment.

Richard Moore, the Michigan man, was sentenced to death because he was convicted of killing a store clerk while committing a robbery. It is a textbook case of what is called a felony murder. Without knowing anything more about the case and never having met the man, I would have accepted the sentence had I not spent time with Mr. Moore. Did he commit a horrible crime that caused endless pain and suffering to many people?

Absolutely.

Is he a horrible person who deserves to die?

That's debatable.

Each time I walk into a convenience store, I think of Richard Moore. I catch myself looking around, conscious of who else is there and what they are doing. My meeting him and learning about him and his crime has had an effect on my behavior and awareness of my surroundings. I have learned that killers don't wear labels identifying them as being capable of a horrific act. Killers don't have a certain look. They come in all shapes, sizes, and colors. Hopefully there will be a day when I don't think about murder upon entering a convenience store, but that day is not today.

The death penalty is a problem in this country whether you're for or against it. If you're for it, you probably think the process is too slow. If you're against it, you probably think it's unconstitutional and inhumane. Regardless of your position, it's wise to put human faces on the players to understand what's at stake. The state intentionally puts to death another human being, and it does so in the name of every citizen it represents. But executing a murderer does not bring back the victims, and it seems to me that allowing the killer to live out their days in prison does not devalue the life of the victim.

"Killing the killer will bring closure for the family," a prosecutor often says. That may be true if the execution takes place within a year or two of the conviction. But dragging out the process for 15, 20, 30, or more years surely has the opposite effect. Every time an appeal is denied or something else happens with the case, the family is told and has to live it all over again. They feel compelled to attend meetings and hearings, and to do interviews about the crime and how they feel about the punishment. They usually watch what unfolds on television news and even come face to face with the offender in court. And this can happen time and again through the years.

There is no closure in that. There is no sense of peace. If families and juries knew how long it takes to get so-called closure, some would seek to get peace of mind some other way — and the sooner the better.

Some victims' loved ones opt to forgive the killer. Forgiveness provides closure. I've thought a lot about this. It's also a fact that some convicted murderers are innocent of the crime. Death row inmates have spent years behind bars awaiting their executions and later are exonerated when critical evidence comes to light. One cannot help but wonder how many innocent people were executed. Conviction is reversible; death is not.

Some very thoughtful people believe that the death penalty is a deterrent to violent crime. However, the murder rate in non-death-penalty states is consistently lower than in states that do execute killers — and the gap has widened since 1990. If it is not a deterrent, why have it?

Appeals are in place to prevent innocent people from being executed. New trials can be granted if judges determine the trials were not conducted properly. Introduction of new and compelling evidence is not unusual. DNA evidence has saved the lives of at least 17 death row inmates since the introduction of samples have been allowed in trials. Forensic science is always evolving. It's time our judicial system does too.

It's also interesting to note that 19 states have abolished the death penalty. There are excellent reasons for this. It's important for each of us to know why. If abolishing the death penalty is not acceptable, then at least members of the public should be granted more access to the living conditions of those who await their fate as well as the way in which the ultimate punishment is carried out.

My first impression of death row was that it was a cold, murky, dangerous, shark-infested pit. I was all eyes and ears while I kept my mouth shut. Upon entering the row my mind was clouded by anxiety and doubt. Sweat poured from my body but failed to wash it out. Would I be eaten alive?

But I learned that most of the killers welcomed me. They generally lived quietly and seemed relaxed. They certainly did not have wonderful accommodations, yet death row was not a living hell. The sharks accepted me; I accepted them. I know a lot more now about living, dying, and respect for humankind. Tony — my fellow prison volunteer — was right: South Carolina's death row was a surprisingly relaxed place.